Voyagers of the Chilcotin
(chil kō'tən)

VOYAGERS
OF THE CHILCOTIN

CAROLYN FOLTZ

ISBN 0-9650963-0-0

Printed in Canada
by Hignell Printing, Winnipeg, Manitoba

Cover design: Tawna Eisworth

In memory of Elijah Gurr
1910-1982

ACKNOWLEDGMENT

My deepest love and appreciation to my husband David for sharing such special memories.

I wish to thank the editor of Coast Mountain News, Angela Hall, for running Voyagers of the Chilcotin as an on-going series. Thanks to Graham Hall for being such a special friend.

I would like to thank my family for their support and enthusiasm: Pam, Chere' and Danny; Grace Shelton, Phyllis Thomas, Johnny and Barbara Thomas, Carmen and Camille Thomas, Bob and Shirley Shelton, Gary and Sandy Shelton, Julie Pogany, George and Cindy Williams.

A special thanks to Isabell Gurr, Mack and Ruth Gurr, Earl and Millie Gurr.

Thanks to Tracey Gillespie.

Contents

Foreword

Far to the north, in the heart of British Columbia, there is a vast untamed region known as the Chilcotin Plateau. Many books have been written about the Chilcotin, along with its early settlers and the extraordinary characters crossing its boundaries. The Chilcotin is a land of mystery and wonderment, the stuff that legends are made of, and the area abounds with wild-eyed yarns and folklore.

With its never-ending sea of jackpine forest, the Chilcotin Plateau depicts an unbridled wilderness. The 15,000 square-mile territory yields wild grassy meadows, poplar thickets, fir-covered ridges, and crystal clear streams. Pristine lakes are too numerous to count, and deep within its inner confines are dank jungles filled with swamps. A rich tapestry of design, the Chilcotin is home for many species of wildlife: the grizzly and black bear, big horned sheep, mountain goat, moose, and deer. For decades, large cattle empires have dominated the Chilcotin realm and countless miles of back country trails have preserved the horse as a way of life.

Etched deep in the land is a road that at one time, was no more than a dirt trail linking

Williams Lake in the east, to Anahim Lake in the west. Beyond Anahim Lake there is a great barrier called the coast mountain range. The citadels act as fortification for a valley revered by most as a paradise. The utopia is called Bella Coola. The remote Valley is home of the Native thunderbird, the great bald eagle.

Located 250 miles north of Vancouver, the Bella Coola Valley is situated in a picturesque fjord that is sixty miles long. The beauty of the inlet port is accentuated by lofty peaks reaching 10,000 feet to the sky. Forty miles in length, the Valley runs east to west and provides a refreshing glimpse of nature at its finest. To the north and south of the Valley lay endless stretches of elevated peaks with huge glacier fields.

Many legends have been molded in remote areas such as the Chilcotin. But one tale stands above the rest, for not a day goes by without the amazing story being told somewhere. The legend goes like this:

Long ago, steamships regularly visited the Bella Coola Harbor providing the only means of transportation in or out, and supplied the local people with commodities. Passenger fares and freight charges were extremely high. Without a link to the interior, Bella Coola was destined to remain in the back washes and eddies of approaching economic development. For families trying to exist on little or no income, it was a constant struggle just to survive.

For decades the people of Bella Coola had petitioned their government to build a road to Anahim Lake only forty-two miles from the Valley floor. The vital connection would provide entry to the Chilcotin Plateau and ultimately to the interior of British Columbia. But government officials continually denied their requests saying it was neither practical nor possible. The rejections cited major obstacles prohibiting a road. The main one being a perpendicular solid rock mountain 6,000 feet high with huge unstable rock slides. The cost of such an engineering feat would be excessive.

The legend says the people of Bella Coola were a unique clan. Most of them were descendants of Norwegian settlers. With the spirit of Vikings running through their veins, they had the inherent ability to survive in a lifestyle that demanded hard work and ingenuity. To them, there was no such thing as an impossible task. If there was a will, they could always find a way.

It is said that in 1947, the people formed a group called the Bella Coola Board of Trade and its members were Cliff Kopas, Elijah (Lige) Gurr, Wally Stiles, Eric Hammer, Norman Saugstad, Mike Christensen, Bill Wright, Wilf Christensen, Andy Widsten, Curtis Urseth, and Ralph Sneyd.

The Board started raising money for a road. A prize-winning steer was donated by Benny Abbott, hotel keeper at Williams Lake, and brought in $400 in raffle money. The Bella Coola Natives staged a weird masked dance raising more money for the project. The Footlights Club at Ocean Falls brought a vaudeville show to Bella Coola and raised $400. Basket socials and honest begging produced further results.

Then, in 1952, a telegram was sent to the Department of Public Works in Victoria:

"This is to advise you that we are going to start immediately building the road from Anahim Lake to Bella Coola."

The legend says that Lige Gurr was sent to seek out the best route for the envisioned road. Lige was a large man with a jovial nature and used to hard work. Right from the beginning, the assignment proved to be difficult. Finally, after much effort, Lige had his strategy all mapped out.

Returning to the Board, Lige explained there was a large basin between Anahim Lake and the rim rock of the Bella Coola Valley. The basin was forty miles around or thirty miles across. Lige wanted to go straight across.

He was told of bottomless swamps and bogholes in the area making it almost impassable. Thomas Squinas, a Native wolf hunter, volunteered to show Lige the best way through the basin.

Next, Lige went to Tatla Lake to talk to Bill Graham, hoping to hire his D6 Cat on an IOU basis. Bill Graham agreed.

Following the blazes put on the trees by Lige, Alf Bracewell was at the controls, and was to build a road 30 miles through the wilderness. Thomas Squinas was to select the high spots, avoiding the worst bogholes and ridges, and Lige was to refine the trail working just ahead of the bulldozer.

The road builders hadn't yet found the best route down the mountainside. Lige suggested following Young Creek, a turbulent stream that began in the Rainbow Mountains, and tumbled down a steep narrow valley. Blondie Swanson, an engineer with Pacific Mills Northern Pulpwood in Ocean Falls scouted the proposed area and agreed with Lige.

Forty-two days after the Bella Coola residents started building their road, the Minister of Highways reserved the modest sum of $50,000 for the project. The Board of Trade quickly bought what was needed and established a base camp at lower Young Creek on the Valley floor.

Foreword

A bulldozer, operated by George Dalshaug, started carving out a road in the solid rock mountain. Now, there were work crews at each end of the project. The base mountain crew had a Cat, two vehicles, a powder monkey, and a couple of men hauling blasting powder by horse.

The men at Anahim Lake had fairly easy going crossing the Chilcotin plateau, but they slowed down considerably when they reached the top of the hill. From there on, there was considerable rock work to be done. On the Bella Coola end, it was rock work right from the start.

Lige had three sons working for the road crews. Mack and Dean worked at the Bella Coola end while Melvin worked as a powder monkey for the Anahim crew.

There was quite a tent community at the base of the hill as the families of the road builders camped with them all summer. The mosquitoes were unbearable. All they could do was build a campfire and sit in the smoke.

The camp tents measured twelve by sixteen feet. The cook house was the same size, but it had a very large stove and a long wooden table used for eating. Cupboards were constructed by stacking empty powder boxes with boards in-between. People sat on empty powder box chairs and there was plenty of them. If company arrived, they were offered a powder box.

The tent community was primitive but comfortable. At first, the toilet facility was no more than a rail between two trees. Eventually, the men built a real outhouse. The outhouse proved to be the only structure in camp the bears didn't want to investigate.

Women with babies had to pack water from a nearby stream so they could wash diapers on a scrub board. A box with a screen door was attached to a board underneath a bridge, acting as a cooler for fresh foods.

Isabell Gurr (Lige's wife) was one of many women who cooked for the road crew. The cook's day started very early and it was quite a chore getting everyone fed. But the real challenge came later. That's when Isabell had to contend with a mother grizzly bear and her two cubs, fishing in a nearby stream. Isabell kept a truck door open with keys in the ignition, just in case she needed to make a fast departure.

Camp life became the normal routine for the men and women working long hours to fulfill a dream. There were great camp cooks like Joe Goff and Louise Mackay who was rated one of the best. The cooks were assisted by local women who helped prepare and deliver food to the workers.

There were people like Norman and Shirley Saugstad, Bert and Peggy Matthews, and Curtis and Louise Urseth who took an arduous journey by horseback to determine if a road was even possible. They traveled through swamps, slides, heavy brush, and were constantly plagued with insects. Blondie Swanson knew a lot about road building which proved to be an invaluable asset. There was Bill Howden, Alger Brynildsen and Morton Svisdahl. Ole Nicoli and George Shriner packed dynamite to the blasters and built bridges by hand.

As the assault on the hill continued, the men often took great chances. The TD18 International bulldozer used by the Bella Coola crew was quite old. Its operator, George Dalshaug, challenged death every day. He moved over rock slides and crossed unstable stretches by anchoring the Cat to large trees. The Cat slipped off the mountain once, and Dalshaug had to jump free. Fortunately, the machine hung up on a rock outcropping fifty feet below. Eventually, the crew winched the Cat back up the mountain.

The powder crew was equipped with two air compressors and a couple of jackhammers. While the construction crew blasted, bulldozed, and chiseled out a trail up the rock wall, dozens of valley residents hauled donated supplies into camp.

Hauling and loading dynamite was very dangerous and not for the faint hearted. On one occasion, Lloyd Brynildsen, Fay Hastings and Melvin Gurr were loading dynamite. After drilling, they loaded up three shots and were ready to light them all at once. They had the proper length of fuse which was four minutes. A visitor, watching them at work, became very excited about the upcoming blast. He started moving away from the blasters at a very fast pace, so Lloyd Brynildsen decided to stir things up a bit. He ran on past the excited fellow and yelled:

"Ninety-nine sticks and they're all on short fuses. Run like hell!"

This stirred things up all right. The crew ran to the back of the Cat for protection, but the terrified visitor ended up diving beneath it, almost knocking himself out.

On another occasion, the blasting crew worked for weeks preparing to blast a massive section of rock. Finally, when the blast took place, the huge chunk lifted high up off its foundation, then plopped right back in place.

In the meantime, Lige kept searching for the best route up the hill. He constantly moved up and down the mountain. He was now working in the roughest terrain imaginable, using an old aneroid barometer and an Abner level that he'd borrowed.

Finally, the road crews were working a half mile apart. Then came word they were out of money until the next fiscal year, seven months away.

Louise MacKay was the first to speak up. She told the workers if they could get some food donated, she would stay and cook. The road crew said they would stay and work if they could have grub to eat. It then became a personal challenge to everyone involved. They kept on working.

At long last, the two Cats were in sight of each other. On that final day, they waited 150 feet apart so spectators could see the uniting of the east with the west. Lige threw his hat in the air and shouted, "Finish it."

It had taken two years just to complete a Cat road from Anahim Lake to the Bella Coola Valley. The crew at the Bella Coola end blasted out five miles in solid rock. The Anahim crew completed thirty-seven miles.

The road was officially opened July 18, 1955. The Minister of Highways, the Honorable P. Gaglardi, was to call the project "magnificent in its conception and astounding in its completion."

The Cat road was just the beginning. Upgrading and maintenance required continued effort. Work crews spent most of their summers at base camp for five years just trying to improve it. They didn't have much equipment, just a couple of Cats, a grader, two trucks, and a loader.

The second year after the road was opened, the decision was made to keep it open in the wintertime. Snow was the big problem. A total of forty-five feet fell one winter, and it was common to have six feet of snow on the ground at any one time. The crew continually shoved snow out of the way, leaving snow banks up to 12 feet high. And, they continued to live in tents while putting up with the 45 degrees below zero weather.

A plaque commemorating the opening of the Bella Coola Road states:

AT THIS SITE ON SEPTEMBER 26TH, 1953
TWO BULLDOZERS
OPERATED BY ALF BRACEWELL AND
GEORGE DALSHAUG TOUCHED BLADES
TO SYMBOLIZE THE OPENING OF A ROAD
THROUGH THE MOUNTAIN BARRIER OF THE
COAST RANGE
MARKED OUT BY ELIJAH GURR
TWO YEARS OF STRENUOUS LOCAL EFFORT
THUS ESTABLISHED A THIRD HIGHWAY ROUTE
ACROSS THIS PROVINCE TO THE PACIFIC OCEAN
THROUGH AN AREA ORIGINALLY EXPLORED
BY LIEUT. H. SPENCER PALMER, R.E. 1862

The legend of the road is as real today as it was almost a half century ago. Today, the road stands as a tribute to the people who built it. The fact that it wasn't engineered or built by a public agency, or by individuals seeking fame or fortune speaks for itself. It is a refreshing thought that a group of people had the insight, as well as the ability, to bring about their own destiny.

Perhaps it was the spirit of the Vikings that spurred them on, or the magic of the gnomes. One thing is certain: They conquered insurmountable odds. And together, they became the voyagers of the Chilcotin.

1

Voyagers of the Chilcotin

Looking out across the vast Sheep Creek Bridge with its shadow falling upon the Fraser River, I couldn't help but feel a sense of excitement. Only 17 miles from Williams Lake, British Columbia, Canada, the bridge connects the two land masses bordering the Fraser River on each side as it moves southward. Most importantly, it provides Canada's third outlet to the Pacific Ocean.

I first saw this bridge in 1961 when its new construction replaced the old structure that ranchers crossed in the early days. Beyond the bridge, an untamed land of spectacular scenery and unique pioneer and Native history mystifies the unsuspecting traveler. It is a land where cowboys still move large cattle herds to better pasture. This spectacular region is called the Chilcotin.

Traveling westerly, the 300 miles of dirt road ultimately ends at the Burke Channel Inlet and a fishing village known as Bella Coola. The last part of the journey can test anyone's fortitude, for between Anahim Lake and Bella Coola (a section laid out and built entirely by local residents) stands "the Hill". The landmark is renown for its 5,000 foot drop in elevation accomplished in 12 linear miles and three switchbacks.

My uncle Lige Gurr, along with many other local residents, were responsible for establishing vehicle travel to the inhabitants of the Bella Coola Valley. They literally blasted out a trail in the rock-rimmed mountain terrain that surrounded the Valley. When residents of the Valley traveled the Chilcotin connection, the route became known as Freedom Road.

The road officially opened in 1955. It was not uncommon in 1961, to still see horse-drawn buckboards hauling Native families as they progressed down the dirt trail. I came to realize that wagon travel made good sense, for a wagon is designed for high-rooted, narrow, twisting dirt roads containing mud holes and washboard-riveted sections.

It was 1961 when my parents, Bud and Grace Shelton, my grandmother Ada Gurr, my 18-year-old brother Gary, my four-year-old sister Cindy, and myself at 16 years old, had the opportunity to caravan with my Uncle Lige and Aunt Isabell across the Chilcotin.

Traversing the road in our 1959 Chevy station wagon, sitting low to the ground, proved to be a challenge. It didn't take long for us to realize that we were outmatched. It took 14 hours to travel the road that day in 1961. We bottomed out several times in bogholes, made car repairs, and developed rattles in the chassis that didn't existed before. We lost the power steering in our Chevy, and eventually all of its shocks became so worn, they later had to be replaced.

We endured the never-ending dust covering everyone and everything with its dry, powdery residue. When our nostrils filled up with dust, we sneezed non-stop. Our eyes became outlined with clay and our mouths formed dirt rings. Our hair took on a gray appearance, becoming weighted down with dirt. Traveling along in our dust dungeon, we resembled something out of a horror movie.

Somewhere on the road we stopped at a creek. A bridge stretched from bank to bank as glimmering rays of sunlight danced on the water. We gladly climbed out of the dusty car, but stirred-up dust made us cough for several minutes before it settled over everything in sight. Seeking refuge from the heat and dust, I crawled beneath the bridge. I dipped cold water from the stream with my hands and generously splashed some on my face. Then I laid back and rested on a clump of grass, closing my eyes. I felt like a troll laying under a bridge and I'm sure I must have resembled one.

Suddenly, there was a pounding on the boards above. It took me several seconds to realize that a team of horses with a buckboard was passing overhead. At that moment, a large buildup of accumulated dirt filtered through the planks landing on my face and inside my shirt. My wet face now took on a marbled mud effect and I looked like a minstrel ready to perform in "black face" with white blaring eyeballs.

Everyone got quite a kick out of my appearance and they were still laughing as we started down the road once more.

Somewhere between Anahim Lake and the Bella Coola Valley, I became carsick. Somehow, I managed to fall asleep. When I awoke several hours later, I noticed a hushed silence in our car. I was informed that we'd descended a gigantic hill with an extremely steep grade. I was still feeling sick so I wasn't too concerned about missing a hill. I just wanted the long dusty trip to come to an end.

And so we finally arrived in the Bella Coola Valley to meet our long-lost relatives. We stayed with Melvin and Elaine Gurr in Hagensborg, and looking as we did, I'm surprised they let us in their home.

In my infinite sixteen-year-old wisdom, I determined right away, we'd become time travelers, and it was 1865. Not one home in the Valley had a television set. Some didn't even have running water or electricity. Many folks used kerosene lamps and outdoor facilities. When we arrived in Bella Coola, we needed to turn our watches back 100 years.

I spent the better part of a week sick to my stomach from the ingested dust on the trip. My illness was overshadowed by the looming fear that the only way back home was to travel the road once again.

Surprisingly, when we traveled back over the relentless, dusty trail, my brother Gary and I realized we had formed a strange attachment to the remote Valley and the Chilcotin. The further away from the Valley we travelled, the more we yearned to return. The return to Bella Coola became a destined dream.

August, 1965

Looking out at the gray-green Fraser River and the Sheep Creek Bridge, once again the sense of adventure and excitement overwhelmed me.

After sitting for three days in the hot crowded cab of a pickup truck, my 22-year-old husband, Dave Foltz, my 13-year-old nephew, Johnny Thomas, and me at 20 years old and five months pregnant, crossed over the metal bridge that linked us with the Chilcotin and our future home. California seemed a long way off as our overweight, fully loaded GMC pickup truck aimed westerly toward its goal of the Bella Coola Valley. The outstretched dirt road loomed before us.

My brother Gary and his wife Sandy made this trip three months ahead of us. They'd found a house to live in and Gary was working in the woods for Crown Zellerbach, a large logging company. The good news was there was a job too, for Dave working in the woods. Dave, born and raised in San Francisco, California, was confident that working in the woods was something he could easily adapt to.

"It can't take 14 hours to go 300 miles," Dave said suspiciously, eyebrows arched. "That would be about 21 miles per hour. I can almost walk that fast!"

Teenager Johnny, nonchalant about Dave's concerns, teased with little quips aimed at Dave. The source of his teasing was due to an experience we'd had while traveling through northern California two days earlier.

"I hope this bumpy road doesn't hurt your sore bottom Uncle Dave. How are you feeling today anyway?"

Johnny quickly turned his head away from us and looked toward the window next to him. I didn't have to see his face to know he was trying to hide a devilish grin on his face. His comment was enough to get a giggle out of me as I remembered Dave's dilemma . . .

The night before we left California, a well-meaning friend had given us a farewell dinner. Something was wrong with the food and we were hit with a terrible case of diarrhea while traveling. Well, I should say, Johnny and I were hit hard, and we had insisted on stopping at every wide spot in the road to use the bathroom. Dave was perturbed with us because our traveling time was constantly being interrupted. He himself seemed fine until somewhere near Red Bluff, California, then the "frizzles" caught up with him. He suddenly sat straight up and veered the truck toward the dirt shoulder.

"What's wrong?" I asked.

"I have to go." The look on his face needed no more explanation. He was in "hurt city" and looking for "a way out of town".

Dave leaped out of the rig and ran around in front. He seemed to be looking for a secluded area, panicked--then ran for the elevated fence line a few yards away. The expression on his face revealed panic and pain. He reached the fence, hoping for a gulch on the other side, but no, the land was flat and this simply elevated him. He still had no place to hide. I thought he would cross over the fence, but instead he continued to grip the barbed wire. I noticed his frozen stance change to awkward disbelief at what was happening to him. Johnny and I looked at each other confirming our suspicions. We heard Dave cussing as he walked slowly back to the truck. I wanted to be helpful so I offered a suggestion.

"Dave, we can turn the truck at an angle so no one can see you. Just go at the side of the road."

"It's too damn late," he said slowly between clenched teeth.

I started to ask, "What do you mean?" But I knew what he meant. What a place to get into trouble. Not even a large rock, bush or tree. Just barren flat land and a temperature of 110 degrees in any shade that could be found.

"Well, ah," I couldn't think what to say.

"Well, ah, nothing. Damn it, I have to change."
"But where?" I questioned.
"Who cares? "

We felt sorry for the poor guy, but, after all, it was a pretty funny sight watching him dig through the back of the truck searching for clean clothes. He never once stopped cussing. Then I heard Johnny snicker.

"Don't you laugh," I warned as my voice cracked with built-up, unreleased laughter trying to break free.

In his totally embarrassed state, Dave decided that nothing really mattered, so he stripped right there along side the road, all the while still cussing. I noticed several vehicles slow down as people glared at the sight alongside the road. Johnny and I could catch fleeting glimpses of occupants in passing vehicles with their mouths wide open.

"I'm not going to laugh," Johnny said matter-of-factly as an unrestrained grin swept his face and tears formed in his eyes. Desperately he tried to hold back the waves of laughter pounding at his chest. A burst of laughter shot through me as I stared into Johnny's face, but quickly subsided as Dave approached the driver's side of the truck. He was still cussing. I swallowed what felt like a giant balloon and fought back surging giggles. Looking straight ahead, I focused on an invisible non-existent object. Johnny turned his head away from me and looked out the window.

"Damn it," Dave said, "I couldn't find any underwear. Just these new Levis that haven't been washed yet."

I managed a weak squeak, "What did you do with the pants you had on?"

"What do you think I did with them? I left them by the side of the road."

I felt Johnny squirm next to me, still facing the window.

"If someone comes along and wants those pants, they can have them," Dave said, as he adjusted the starchy crotch. (New blue jeans in those days were stiff as a board, and required many washings to soften them to the comfortable stage--not at all like the ones we can buy now.)

Dave lifted himself into the cab and sat gently on the seat. Johnny and I both looked over at him.

"Those pants look a little stiff," Johnny said, his voice wavering.

Dave surveyed the situation in the cab. I turned and stared straight ahead without a trace of the smile that was fighting to break through. Johnny faced the window, but his whole body was shaking.

"If either of you laugh, I'll . . ." Dave sounded just a little perturbed.

Somehow, we managed to travel on down the road disguising any hint of laughter. Johnny looked out the window, and I sat frozen in place facing the windshield. Once in a while I coughed to release built-up energy. And poor Dave, between the starchy Levis and lack of clean-up material, he got to experience a whole new meaning of the word "chafed."

Two days later, as we approached the Sheep Creek Hill with the Fraser River behind us, Dave's spirits were lifted and his good humor returned. He simply replied to Johnny's concern:

"Don't be worried about my sore bottom on this bumpy road. We're going to make this trip across the Chilcotin in record time. It won't take us 14 hours to travel 300 miles."

Sheep Creek Hill was extremely steep with a total of 33 switchbacks and an 18% grade. The washboard effect caused by rain and ruts resembled the same sensation as trying to drive up a creek bed. The truck bounced and twisted as we climbed up the snake-like trail. Any kind of speed was impossible because the truck constantly fishtailed to the outer edge of the powdery berm.

It was difficult at best for three people in a truck cab, with a food chest taking up valuable floor space, to travel. But the real clincher was a heater that never shut off. No matter what we tried, warm air constantly poured out from the heater vent. On that 18th day of August, we really didn't need any more heat. We traveled with the windows down to compensate for the hot air, and as a result, the cab was layered in dust and dirt. We constantly tried to keep balanced while completing horseshoe turns, but were jolted back and forth colliding with each other.

After two hours, we reached Riske Creek and pulled up to a small old-fashioned gas pump to fuel up. We sat staring straight ahead for one peaceful, non-vibrating moment. Dave checked the odometer. We had travelled 35 miles into the Chilcotin.

"Okay, how much further is this Bella Coola?" Dave asked, with a grumpy stare aimed at me.

"About 265 miles," was my cheerful response.

Dave shook his head. "This truck will never make it. It gets to shaking so bad, I expect to see pieces of it falling off as I drive down the road. It will be totally destroyed by the time we arrive in

Bella Coola. This road better get a whole lot better than what we've seen."

"We'll probably be able to travel a lot faster now that we're up on top. No more switchbacks," I explained.

We soon left Riske Creek and gradually increased our speed.

"Boy, we're making good time now," Dave said, with an encouraging look on his face.

The speedometer displayed 30 mph.

All of a sudden, "Rat-ta-tat-tat, rat-ta-tat-tat," as the truck entered a series of washboard rippled ruts and the truck fishtailed. Dave tapped the brakes and BOOM! We bottomed out on high walls of dried ruts remaining from a once-stuck vehicle. Then, smooshsh! We entered a watery boghole.

We learned the hard way, never to slow down when entering a boghole. Once speed was lost, there was no hope of seeing dry ground again. As we fought to break free of the gushy stuff, I envisioned sunken vehicles buried in bottomless pits of mud, their inhabitants never heard of again. Then, the truck started to move. It slipped and slid while gradually inching its way forward. Finally, we were free. Looking back, I could see that we left deep grooves for the boghole's next victim.

We gained another 15 miles on the road. Then, a tire blew, and a seized-up wheel bearing caused extensive damage to the right-rear braking system. To make matters worse, we discovered the GMC truck, purchased just before our trip, didn't have a tire iron on board. This meant we couldn't even remove the tire. We'd replaced all the old tires with new before leaving

California, spending $200 in the process, and hadn't expected any tire problems.

"I can't even get the tire off unless someone comes along and stops to helps us," Dave complained. "And I don't have a clue where the nearest service station is from here."

Dave looked toward the setting sun as evening settled down around us.

The first passer-by was a farmer with a team of horses pulling a hay wagon. He was heading east toward Williams Lake. The farmer offered us a ride, and even though the soft hay did look inviting, we stood united in the decision not to give up one inch of the road to backtrack.

We built a fire 25 yards away from the injured truck and close to the jackpine forest. I pulled out some old blankets from the back of the truck as the temperature started to cool rapidly.

An hour later, a man in a pickup truck stopped and offered to help. We were relieved to hear that he owned a tire iron, and the men soon removed the wheel. It became obvious that we needed to replace the wheel bearing and fix the damaged braking system.

After a lot of speculation, Dave drove off with the stranger who'd convinced him that somewhere, out across the Chilcotin, in a barn or a shed, there would be a wheel bearing for the nine-year-old truck.

Johnny and I walked slowly to our campfire and watched as Dave disappeared down the road. I couldn't help but wonder when, or if, I would ever see him again. I carried Dave's .22 pistol cradled in its holster. Looking at it, I wondered if it would kill anything bigger than a jackrabbit. I knew we were in grizzly bear country and I felt more than a little nervous.

Johnny and I sat around the campfire and ate what remained of our food: three cinnamon rolls and a bag of shelled peanuts. We wrapped up in blankets as the air turned cold.

At midnight we still gazed into the flames of the fire, unable to sleep. We told stories and sang church songs. During one of the breaks in verse, I became aware of a series of sounds coming from a short stand of trees just left of our camp. I was sure Johnny heard them too, as we both tried to out sing the other, all the time hoping the noise would stop. But it didn't.

"There is something in the trees," Johnny said looking directly at me.

Silence filled the air. We sat motionless and listened.

"Hello the camp," an unfamiliar voice rang out.

"Hello," we both yelled back at the same time.

A young Native man, probably in his 20's, stepped out from the trees. He was leading a horse by its reins.

With relief, we welcomed him to our camp. We learned that a cattle drive, somewhere in the area, had left him behind on the trail. He'd followed the light of our campfire from across the valley hoping to catch up with the wranglers and the herd.

Johnny and I felt a sense of comfort meeting the local man, and he seemed relieved to find a campfire. He told us he'd be happy to join us during our long vigil. We were more than happy to share what was left of the shelled peanuts, and soon we were swapping stories.

The man was of the Ulkatcho Native people and had been born and raised on the Chilcotin. He'd never traveled any further than Williams Lake to the east, or Bella Coola to the west. He was very familiar with the Bella Coola Valley because his family traveled there each summer to catch salmon. He was a little surprised to learn that we would be staying on in the Valley, instead of returning to California.

Sometime around 5:00 a.m., Dave returned with the stranger. They'd been gone over ten hours going from shed to shed, barn to barn, across the Chilcotin, and had managed to find exactly what they needed to make the repairs. We were ecstatic!

At 8:00 a.m., we were ready to travel once more with a renewed confidence that anything could be conquered. We positioned ourselves in the tight confined quarters of the truck cab with its filthy interior. By all appearances we looked alert, considering everything.

We waved good-bye to the stranger, who refused any monetary compensation. Saying good-bye, Johnny and I were thankful for the Native man, who'd been our companion and friend during our long night on the Chilcotin. We'd been formally introduced to the "charity of the Chilcotin".

We soon passed by Lee's Corner, a wide spot in the road with a small store. Dave explained that he and the stranger had stopped in Lee's Corner. Dave had rummaged through endless amounts of auto parts in old sheds, and was shocked when he discovered the exact wheel bearing he needed for the truck. At least that problem was solved. But the old bearing had to be removed from the axle. On to another shed where the stranger produced a torch. They soon had it fired up, cut the old bearing off, then fitted the new one onto the axle.

Johnny and I listened to Dave's amazing story. We wondered where we'd be, if the man had never stopped.

"Rat-ta-tat-tat, rat-ta-tat-tat," we fishtailed as Dave hit the brake. Then BOOM! We bottomed out but picked up speed as smooshsh! We inched through another watery boghole.

We had traveled 20 miles in one hour when exhaustion took over and we had to stop. The three of us leaned on one another while we slept in the dust-filled cab.

We were on the road again by 11:00 a.m. traveling a few miles further. We stopped in Redstone, another wide spot in the road with a store and a house.

We ate breakfast in the kitchen of the store owner, a nice lady who cooked a wonderful meal. The woman explained that she longed to visit California, the land of sunshine and beautiful beaches. She was tired of the cold Chilcotin plateau with its unpredictable weather and endless bogholes.

"How cold does it get here?" Dave asked.

"The record is 70 degrees below zero."

Stunned by the news, Dave dropped his fork on the floor.

When we finished eating, Dave fueled up the truck using an old-fashioned gravity-fed method. It was the first time we'd ever seen such a contraption. First, Dave pumped a handle that filled a cylinder, made of glass, with fuel. The container had markings in gallon increments, and when Dave filled it to the desired amount, he stopped pumping. Then, a hose was used to feed the fuel into our tank. This method was used in places across the Chilcotin where there was no electricity to operate a pump.

We started down the dusty trail once more and felt confident we were making good time as the speedometer displayed 25 mph. This foolhardy notion was dashed when, the all too familiar, "Rat-ta-tat-tat, rat-ta-tat-tat," and we fishtailed. Dave hit the brake. Then BOOM! We bottomed out but picked up speed as smooshsh! We inched through yet another boghole.

It was possible to watch for miles ahead the dreaded cloud of dust announcing an approaching vehicle. I found it interesting that when the occupants of the vehicle came into view, they always waved to us. It was an apologetic gesture for the inevitable blinding blast of dust and rocks to follow.

We gained a few more miles before our next flat tire.

"Where are you kids from?" The local Chilcotinite asked, as he loaned Dave his tire iron.

"California."

That seemed to explain "everything". If there hadn't been so much dust covering the truck license plate, he wouldn't have to ask.

Our next stop was Tatla Lake where we fueled up and repaired the tire. A sign advertising an old hotel promised clean rooms and hot baths. A generator blared loudly providing the only electrical current for miles. I did so wish we could stay, but our finances were low. Our money had been cut short with an unexpected duty fee of $200, which was assessed on our truck at the Canadian border. This was due to the fact we hadn't owned our truck six months prior to becoming landed immigrants.

Once again on the road, we traveled 20 more miles before our next flat tire. While the guys waited for help to come along, I was instantly drawn to a little lake just a few steps away from the road. I couldn't wait to clean up.

I rolled up my pant legs and submerged my dirt-stained legs into the icy water. I dipped a wash cloth in the water and cleaned off a layer of dirt from my face. Then I washed my neck and arms. My water-soaked legs felt numb by the time I finished my wash-up.

I laid a towel next to me on the ground, in preparation to dry my legs. When I drew them up from the water, I noticed purple-red things attached to my skin. I had never met a leech before, but there are some things in this life that need no introduction. In my horror, I pulled and scraped while removing the ugly little slimy creatures from my legs. Finally, I managed to walk back to the truck.

With the tire change completed, we bid adieu to the local man who was still shaking his head when we drove away. We were happy just to be moving down the road once again.

In an area known as Kleena Kleene the road meandered through large grassy meadows. We pulled over to the side of the road and sat staring in awe at the beautiful coastal mountains across the horizon--part of the Bella Coola range. Our spirits were instantly lifted while envisioning our future home. We drove on toward the glacier-covered monoliths.

In our mirthful, determined state, we began to laugh at our ghostly appearance with eyes defined by blackened circles and dust-caked eye lashes.

"I wonder if this ring-around-the-lip look will ever catch on," Johnny joked.

Dave and I took notice of Johnny's puckered lips, and laughed.

Then, "Rat-ta-tat-tat, rat-ta-tat-tat," and we fishtailed as Dave hit the brake. Then BOOM! We bottomed out but picked up speed as we inched, once more, through a watery boghole.

We had been on the Chilcotin road for twenty-four hours when we repaired another tire at someone's shed.

Another hour of travel and we reached Anahim Lake. After fueling up Dave asked how much money we had left, so I checked my wallet.

"Ten bucks," I reported.

"Thanks to the good ol' duty tariff," Dave said with a smirk. "We better give Gary a call. We still have 80 miles to go to get to his place."

We found out that we could do a radio call from Anahim Lake to Hagensborg to the home of Mack Gurr, Provincial Road Foreman (also my cousin). He in turn could get a message to Gary, who didn't have a phone--if all went well.

Our message went like this: The Foltz' are coming in from Anahim Lake. Try to meet us at the Hill. We've had numerous flat tires and truck repairs.

We left out the part about being broke.

We left Anahim Lake and drove toward the coast mountain range. Before long, a visible change took place in a terrain that now produced weather-worn trees, in a harsh landscape. The tree-lined road soon diminished into a one-lane path. I was sure we'd taken the wrong road, but there was only one road to take.

We crossed several streams with planks for bridges and moved slowly while creeping through a large herd of cattle sharing the road.

Then we hit the roughest road yet.

"Rat-ta-tat-tat, rat-ta-tat-tat," and we fishtailed. Then BOOM! We bottomed out. Smooshsh! This went on for what seemed like an eternity. It took two hours to travel 30 miles.

We were so tired at this point, we started to growl at each other like injured wolves in a pack. I wondered how many divorces had been mentally planned out, while traveling this endless trail, as I looked over at the grumpy old stranger sitting next to me called Dave.

It seemed as though the road would never end, and we were destined to drive into oblivion on the Chilcotin trail. I longed for clean clothes, a bath and to wash my dust-ridden hair. But most of all, I was ready for some different company.

At our wits' end and ready to give up, we turned a corner and there sat Gary and Sandy in their white Econoline van. They'd gotten our message.

We all stood in the middle of the road while they laughed at the way we looked. We didn't worry about traffic because we hadn't seen another vehicle for over two hours. Johnny seemed to liven right up when he met the 13-year old Bella Coola girl traveling with Gary and Sandy. Barbara Gurr had been the one to deliver our message.

We prepared to leave. At the last minute, Johnny decided it was important to "free up" valuable passenger space in our truck, so he rode with the Bella Coola Sheltons, sitting next to his third cousin, Barbara.

We started down the Hill.

For anyone who can't imagine what an 18% descent on a one-lane, chiseled-out-of-rock trail is like, I can tell you it's similar to the scariest carnival ride you've ever ridden.

27

I literally held my breath for two miles. I tried to apply non-existing brakes from the passenger side. Longing for level ground, we continued to move ever so slowly in a slanting, downward motion. I peered out over the edge that should have had guard rail protection only to see a bottomless canyon below. Neither of us dared to speak. We just held our breath and hoped that we would make it safely to the bottom.

At the last horseshoe curved switchback, we all stopped to let the brakes cool down. Gary noticed that Dave appeared dangerously exhausted, so he insisted that Dave ride in the van for the rest of the trip. Sandy could drive the van, while Gary would drive our truck.

We descended the final (and steepest) portion of the Hill. Just before we reached the bottom, the brakes on the truck seemed to fail, and we quickly tapped into the bumper on the van ahead of us. Fortunately, the brakes on the van held firm, and we soon arrived safely at the bottom.

"Now just a couple of hours and you'll be home," Gary cheerfully announced as we passed over Lower Young Creek bridge. "You're in the Bella Coola Valley."

"I can't wait to take a bath," I drawled through dry lips, half dazed, thirty-three hours, and 260 miles later.

"We're making good time now," Gary announced.

I didn't change my blank stare, nor did I look in the direction of the speedometer as..."Rat-ta-tat-tat, rat-ta-tat-tat," and we fishtailed. Then BOOM! We bottomed out but picked up speed as we inched through a watery boghole.

I looked out the dust covered window next to me. Suddenly, I realized how small and insignificant I felt compared to the giant mountains hovering over me. I saw cascading waterfalls pouring from high cliffs. Eventually, they formed creeks and streams that wound through lavish vegetation with a rhythmic energy.

"This is the Bella Coola Valley," I told myself, overwhelmed by its beauty. "This is where my children will be born."

We had endured the long trip across the Chilcotin. That was the price. The Bella Coola Valley was the reward. I knew that each bump, every dusty mile, all the bogholes, and even the Hill--had all been worth it!

2

Valley Newcomers

There was no doubt in my mind, Bella Coola Valley was the most beautiful place on earth. Sheltered by majestic peaks, the Valley was a sanctuary to many forms of plant and animal life. This wonderful collision of nature created a sense of freshness and purity that was beyond belief.

The Bella Coola River, winding through great stands of timber, nurtured many species of spawning salmon; Chinook, (also referred to as King or Spring), Chum, Pink, and Coho, as well as steelhead, Dolly Varden, and cutthroat trout. This great river, with its volumes of fish, yielded some of the greatest sports fishing in the world.

Indigenous species of Hemlock, Douglas Fir, Western Red Cedar, and Spruce grew in abundance. The Valley also provided the occasional Yellow Cedar and Pine.

Varied species of wildlife roamed the forest and mountains: blacktail deer, moose, mountain goat, black bear, grizzly bear, wolf, beaver, river otter, weasel, fox, and cougar. And there were bald eagles galore!

Sitting at sea level, the Valley provided an average temperature of 72 degrees in July; 32 degrees in January. (Little did we know, there would be nothing average or normal about the next two seasons.)

Dave, Johnny and I moved into a Crown Zellerbach house with Gary and Sandy and their two children, Debbie five years old, and Clint, three. The two-story house had four bedrooms, one bathroom, and provided a comfortable atmosphere for our combined families. We were happy just to have a roof over our heads because rentals were very scarce.

Newcomers were a rare breed in Bella Coola in those days and we soon became the focus of many curious on-lookers who wanted to know more about us. We explained that were related to the Mechams and the Gurrs.

The Mecham family had moved to Bella Coola in 1928, and a young 18-year-old Lige Gurr had traveled with them all the way from Utah to help with the move. Along the way, Lige and Isabell Mecham decided to get married and stayed over in Vancouver. When the couple arrived in Bella Coola by boat for a visit, Lige was amazed at the dense coastal valley with its high mountains rising to the sky. Looking up, all he could say was, "There is nowhere to go but up."

The visit to Bella Coola Valley turned into a long one--31 years. During that time, there were seven children born to the couple: Mack, in 1929, Dean, in 1930, Melvin, in 1932, Douglas, in 1934, Buddy, 1936, Betty Jean, in 1937, and Lamont, in 1941.

The main industry in those days was fishing. Canneries were a common site throughout the Burke Channel Inlet. In the Valley there were opportunities in logging, farming, and saw milling.

There was lots of road work and bridge building in progress during the early years to extend the dirt trail up the valley. The difficult work was carried out by using horses, scrapers, and wheelbarrows.

Bella Coola proved to be a good place to live. It was quiet, provided good soil for farming, had lots of fishing, hunting, and game birds that were available all year. People didn't have many luxuries, but they did have the necessities. Neighbors relied upon each other and there was a great communication between them. If someone needed help, a neighbor was always there.

Lige was appointed Public Works Foreman for the Bella Coola Valley in 1954. Upon his transfer to the Williams Lake district in 1959, his son Mack followed in his footsteps becoming foreman. In Williams Lake, Lige worked as a Senior Foreman and was transferred there to straighten out problems that had developed in the local district. He later became Superintendent of the Sheep Creek Hill road project, a vital link to the Chilcotin. Even though they no longer lived in the Valley, Lige and Isabell returned often to visit with their family and friends.

Isabell's brothers and sisters all lived in the Valley. They were Jim, Lewis, Floyd, Albert, and DeLoy Mecham. Her sisters were Myrtle McLean, Thelma Bryant, Edith Ratcliff, and Leora White. In addition to Isabell's family, the couple had five married children of their own still living in the Valley. Somehow, they always managed to stop by the Crown Zellerbach house to see how the newcomer relatives were doing. With other relatives inevitably showing up, we soon had the makings of a good old-fashioned family reunion.

Lige came from a family of wonderful story tellers, and being the adventuresome people that they were, he had wonderful true-life experiences to tell that would hold everyone's interest for hours. Most of his stories were humorous. Whenever Lige was telling one, he'd stop in the middle of the story, long before it was over, and start laughing. His eyes always welled-up with tears, and his whole face rounded out displaying his jovial nature. When Lige laughed, it was like a clap of thunder, and those hearing it had to join in laughing, too. When his story was finally finished, including the punch line, everyone laughed all over again.

Isabell had a soft-spoken manner and a twinkle in her eye. While listening to one of Lige's stories, her brown eyes always appeared larger than normal. When she joined in with the laughter, it sounded like a soft, unruffled giggle.

Lige had two brothers, Earl and DeLoy, as well as two sisters, Grace (my mother) and Helen. They had all been raised in the eastern part of Utah. Their parents, Jimmy and Ada Gurr, were two wonderful people who were well-known for their singing talents, as well as winning many waltzing competitions. The Gurr children were also musically talented, and while in their teens, the boys each played in their own orchestra. Lige played several instruments including the piano, violin, guitar, banjo, and trombone.

Isabell enjoyed knitting, crocheting, and sewing. The long winter nights were spent sitting by the air-tight heater with a gas light burning while Lige read to her. Lige liked hunting and fishing, but he also knitted right along side of Isabell, completing many socks, toques, and sweaters. In the early days, the couple produced their own wool.

How we enjoyed those family gatherings and hearing about the early days in Bella Coola. When it was time for everyone to leave, we could hardly wait for the next family gathering. In the meantime, we all became very industrious.

Nephew Johnny's musical talents soon brought new found interests to the young people in the Valley when he formed a band. He became guitar and drum instructor, while Gary, also an accomplished musician, taught lessons as well. Most of the practice sessions took place in Johnny's upstairs room. The room quickly became a beehive of activity as kids from all over the Valley stopped in after school to practice, or just to listen. Some of the more regular visitors were Barbara Gurr, the three Gurr brothers Daryl, Mike and Brian, Tony and Jay Norton, Keith Mecham, Susan White, and Doug Pelton.

Gary and Dave concentrated on the dangerous profession of logging while making a living, and Sandy and I tried to become efficient in the art of homemaking. Learning to can fruit and vegetables, bake bread, embroider, crochet, and knit was a full-time job. I was still learning the basics when it came to cooking! Sandy and I made a commitment to become as talented a homemaker as our counterparts in the Valley. We wanted to learn the old-style homemaking.

Sandy and I both wore moderate amounts of make-up, but by contrast to the other local women, we stood out as having "painted faces" because they wore none. Gary and Dave suggested that perhaps we didn't need any make-up and should return to a more natural look. Sandy had dark hair and eyes and a beautiful cameo complexion. But I, on the other-hand, had blonde hair, blue eyes and pale skin. If I wanted any color at all, I needed make-up. After agreeing to a two-day, make-up-free-face trial, everyone agreed unanimously that perhaps I was better off to continue with the enhancement of color. I rested my case.

Each morning Sandy and I arose about 5:00 a.m., got the oil stove warmed up, and cooked breakfast. Our logger husbands insisted they needed a large cooked meal to start the day. Sandy usually cooked breakfast while I made sandwiches for the enormous lunches they would take with them.

It was difficult for us to be awake and alert while doing these morning rituals. One morning, as I slapped the meat on the bread, I accidentally picked up a picture of a piece of salami on the package wrapper. I placed it on the bread, covered it with mayonnaise, set another piece of bread over it, and wrapped the paper-meat sandwich in waxed paper.

Later that day, much to my chagrin, a very hungry Dave sank his teeth into what appeared to be a salami sandwich, and ended up spitting out chunks of a picture of meat. The two loggers never let me forget this one small infraction.

Over the holidays I tried to bake a mincemeat pie. Sandy and I disagreed on the crust recipe. She insisted I should use shortening. I told her my mother always used oil. What I didn't realize was my Mom's recipe used both oil and shortening in carefully measured amounts. I stood firm and substituted oil for the shortening called for in the recipe.

When my cousin Mack stopped by with his family, I was delighted that he wanted mincemeat pie for dessert--my mincemeat pie. I tried to sink a sharp knife into the crust to cut a piece, but couldn't even make a dent in the tough surface. It took several minutes to chisel out what resembled a wedge. I quickly covered it with whipping cream, hoping that no one would notice the crust had a problem. Later, when we cleaned the kitchen, we found the plate that had held the mincemeat pie. The internal ingredients had been hollowed out of the impenetrable shell and it looked so strange, the guys really got a good laugh over it. Naturally, they had several smirky remarks regarding my pie that lasted for days.

A week later, Dave and Gary had the nerve to place a note in the middle of my freshly baked homemade bread that hadn't risen properly. The note said, "NICE TRY". The little prankster attitudes of the male minds in our home was beginning to get on my nerves. Inadvertently, I found a way to get even.

It had become a common practice to play "bear scare" every time we went into the outdoors. The men had successfully managed to frighten us women on several different occasions.

One Saturday, Sandy and I took the two kids, Debbie and Clint, up the valley to pick green beans in Vera Mecham's garden near the river. Climbing out of the truck we were instantly aware of a horrible stench, one that only a salmon-eating bear can produce, and the air was pungent with the odor. Vera's dog was accompanying us and started barking wildly. At first, we were a little hesitant to pick beans too far from the truck, but, after a little time had passed, we ventured out further and further down the rows of ripened vegetables. Suddenly, there was a loud noise and thrashing coming from the bushes, and the dog ran toward the sound.

I panicked. Leaping for the kids, I grabbed Debbie under one arm, Clint under the other, and ran as fast as my seven-month pregnant body would allow, with a kid secured at each side. Sandy stood motionless thinking that perhaps it really wasn't a threatening bear who was the perpetrator.

Sure enough, Dave, Gary and Johnny had sneaked up to the garden just to play one of their famous bear pranks on unsuspecting us. When the three pranksters came out of the bushes, they were all but rolling on the ground with laughter because of my reaction. But suddenly, their 'bear scare' was diminished, in comparison to the 'pregnant lady scare' that ensued after my 80-foot-dash for the truck.

Right then, it was agreed by all, that there would be no more pranks. A memorable impression had been formed that a pregnant lady should never be upset--after all, who wanted to be the one to deliver an early baby?

I couldn't help taking advantage of the situation, so, I decided to milk it for awhile. It gave me great satisfaction seeing a little fear on their faces, and I had a real good time during the pampering period that followed.

It was during this time that Johnny became the focus of the male taunting, especially during wrestling matches that usually took place on the living room floor. While visiting with friends, Johnny took pure delight in showing the ten finger-sized bruises across his chest that perfectly matched Uncle Dave's hand. Then, on the inside of his arms, were the round bruises from countering Uncle Gary's karate blows.

The wrestling matches infuriated Sandy. It was quite a sight when Sandy, all five feet of her, warned Gary, who was six feet three inches tall, about the twelve (she counted them) tears in her braided living room rug. But Sandy was quite capable of getting her point across, and the guys had to find a new place to wrestle.

The stairwell in the Crown Zellerbach house didn't have a light. Anyone going upstairs at night climbed them in the dark. At the top of the stairs was a light switch for the room where Dave and I slept. Johnny's room was just off from ours.

Just before Johnny went to bed one night, Gary sneaked up the darkened stairs and hid. When the unsuspecting teenager reached the top of the stairs and went to turn on the light, he was greeted with a blood curdling scream.

To get even, Johnny sneaked down the stairs while Gary was asleep, took his Levis and put them in the freezer. The next morning, Johnny sneaked back down the stairs, at the break of day, and replaced the frozen pants at the foot of Gary's bed.

It seemed we never lacked for entertainment with all the activities going on in our house. As time went by, we became more and more settled in the Valley, establishing new friends, and enjoying our relatives. Mack and Ruth Gurr, with their five children, visited often. We, in turn, visited at their home and took part in family music sessions. Mack could really play the piano and we all enjoyed the homespun attitude of the old family-value system that hadn't, as yet, been corrupted by the invasion of television.

The Gurr children had a naive, innocent charm. For those who love to tease, it was just too inviting. One evening when Mack and Ruth were visiting with their family, I suddenly realized the three boys were sitting cross-legged on the floor, silently staring straight ahead. The source of their amusement was the blank screen of the television that Gary and Sandy brought with them from California. It was the only television in the Valley, and was totally useless, because the high mountains blocked any possible reception. For most people, seeing a television in our home was a first-time experience. Children often asked many questions about the type of picture the TV projected. It was just too difficult to imagine people on a screen in the living room.

"What are you boys staring at?" I asked.

In a Norwegian accent, eleven-year-old Daryl replied, "Gary said that if we watched long enough, we would see TV people."

I turned to look at prankster Gary who sat watching the boys from a distance with a twinkle in his eye and a grin on his face, still carrying on a conversation with Mack.

Even Dave tried calling the boys Curly, Moe and Larry once, referring to the three stooges, but this didn't get a rise out of them. They had no idea who those characters were.

"Good thing your mom and dad didn't name you Ty-Gurr, Vinny-Gurr, or Me-Gurr," teased Dave. The Gurr boys smiled and thought that was pretty funny.

Mack, a delightful combination of intelligence and wit, had the contagious bold laughter so common to the Gurrs. We enjoyed all their visits immensely.

Everyone in Canada had a problem with the name Foltz, and for that matter, the name Carolyn. It took me a long time, and many spellings to realize that the Canadian sound for z is zed, and Carolyn is pronounced Caroline. I soon learned to spell with a zed instead of a z, and answer to the name Caroline. My new Canadian name was Caroline Folt-zed.

Dave and Gary continued to work in the woods and learned to speak the logger's lingo while performing the difficult work. Working for Crown Zellerbach, one of their first assignments was to survey a logging road that would establish an operation in South Bentinck. The site was in a remote uninhabited inlet 40 miles south of Bella Coola. The harsh terrain produced dense tangles of brush intertwined with fallen trees, making survey work next to impossible. Worse still, giant grizzlies and huge black bears roamed the area. The two men earned a whopping $19 a day while doing difficult survey work in the bear-infested area.

Crown Zellerbach purchased a new D-8 bulldozer and low boy trailer for the logging operation at South Bentinck. Both were loaded on a huge steel barge along with trucks and enough equipment and tools to set up a service garage. When a tugboat pulled away from the Bella Coola dock with the barge in-tow, the water was calm and smooth. The weather outlook was fairly good with only a slight chance of showers. The tugboat skipper navigated the Burke Channel just fine. Then suddenly, the wind picked up and the weather turned real ugly. Unable to complete a turn toward the calmer waters of the South Bentinck arm, the in-tow barge took a sudden roll. All the skipper could do was watch, as the nightmare unfolded. The equipment, secured and chained to the deck, instantly broke loose and disappeared beneath the icy waters, never to be seen again.

The expensive mishap in the inlet, along with the difficult survey work, left a formidable impression on Gary and Dave. They'd learned just how hazardous a logging operation could be, even in the beginning stages.

I constantly reminded the guys to be extremely careful while working in the woods. I worried more about bear attacks than anything else, but I also knew that working in the woods presented its own kind of danger. Somehow, I had an unpleasant feeling that something awful was about to happen. I didn't know how, or when, but I just knew.

It was a beautiful Saturday morning when Dave, Gary and Johnny collected their fishing gear for a trip to the Saloompt Bridge.

"Be sure you get back in time to join us at the church for supper this evening," Sandy told the fishermen.

The guys quickly answered they would, then piled into the truck. Dave was driving, Johnny was in the middle, and Gary was next to the passenger window. The men headed down the road for Saloompt Valley and soon decided to check on Uncle Lige and Cousin Mack who were fishing for coho on the south side of the river. Arriving in Saloompt, they turned onto an old logging road that was overgrown with shrubs and trees.

The old trail led to the fishing hole where the two anglers were fishing. After visiting for a short time, the three men departed going back out the same dirt trail. Driving along, they noticed that someone had chopped at the undergrowth to clear the road. There were several pointed branches strewn about.

Suddenly, the truck's extended driver-side mirror caught a large birch sapling that had been chopped to a fine point. Two inches in diameter, the trapped sapling veered through the window-wing and crashed upward striking Dave in the face. As it impacted, it pushed Dave's head to the back of the cab against the rear window. Simultaneously, Dave hit the brake. This reactionary act of braking probably saved his life.

While the startled threesome groped, Dave managed to slide his hand down to the gear shift and place it in reverse. His foot quickly tapped the gas pedal. The pressure subsided as the sapling became dislodged. Dave's head was free, but blood was spewing everywhere.

Quickly, Gary leaned toward Dave to examine the injury. He could see that Dave's nose had been savagely torn open, leaving a gaping wound with one severed nostril dangling by the skin. Gary grabbed Johnny's T-shirt and tore it off of him. He placed it over the injured area. He told Johnny, "Hold it firmly in place and don't let him look in the mirror."

Gary then ran around to the driver's side of the truck. He removed the sapling from the mirror and slid into the driver's position. Dave slid toward Johnny, and the once white T-shirt quickly changed to red.

Gary drove the trail carefully, not wanting another incident. The paved Saloompt road was a welcome sight, but they still had fifteen miles to go to get to a Bella Coola doctor. It took approximately twenty minutes to get to the townsite, and Johnny continued to apply pressure the whole time with the shirt. Dave was still dazed and numb when they arrived at the hospital. They quickly took him in to the emergency room.

Dr. Dave Crosby was a young man in his twenties, and new to the Valley. He examined the wound and informed Gary and Johnny it would take a few hours to suture the nose back together. When Dave was somewhat stabilized, the doctor prepared the needle that would deaden the facial area around the nose. Dave was still coherent when he started injecting the local anesthesia.

Dr. Crosby had an unusual sense of humor. Leaning over his patient, he said, "Dave, you're not going to believe this, but I've always wanted to try a repair job of this nature."

"So glad to oblige," Dave groaned through numbed lips.

The surgery took two hours, and a total of 50 stitches. Most of the stitches were on the inside of the nose, but several were on the outside as well.

When Dr. Crosby was finished, he considered the nose job a work of art.

Dave was placed in a room to rest for the night, while Gary and Johnny returned home. The guys needed to clean up the truck and themselves before joining Sandy and I at the church. Johnny decided to remain at home. He'd had enough excitement for one day.

An hour later, Gary walked into the Hagensborg church. He'd already decided he didn't want another 'pregnant lady scare'. He chose his words very carefully while informing me he would take me to Bella Coola to see Dave.

"What happened?" I asked with concern.

"Oh, he just scratched his nose on a stick. He might need the doctor to look at it."

When we arrived at Dave's room at the hospital, I knew that nothing could have prepared me for his appearance. The swollen, nasty-looking form that protruded from his face was too sickening to look at. The stick collision had blackened both of his eyes. The brownish-red skin surrounding his nose was laced with sutures. If I hadn't know it was him, I wouldn't have recognized my own husband.

Upon our return home with the injured Dave, we all had to deal with the realization that this beautiful, wondrous country was also very dangerous. We were haunted by this fact each time we looked at Dave's horrible-looking face.

As word spread about the bizarre accident, we were inundated with visitors who brought with them horror stories of previous injuries and accidents. Most of the accidents centered around logging.

There were stories of loggers who'd been killed by "widow makers" falling from nowhere. These poor souls had been struck by undetected, rotten limbs that had toppled down on them as they worked. We learned of fallers who'd been struck by branches from adjoining trees surrounding the fallen one. There were men who'd been crushed when logs rolled on them, or cables snapped. We noticed that most men were missing at least one finger, and sometimes even more, from a mishap with an ax. Story after story only heightened our awareness that we were living in a very dangerous country.

We learned that even Uncle Lige had been seriously injured in the 1940's. An old-time steam donkey, that he was operating, suddenly up-ended when a chasing line snapped. Before he knew what happened, he was flung down a hill and buried beneath the framework of the donkey platform. The accident was a serious one, giving him a concussion, several broken ribs and a dislocated shoulder. Lige was rushed to the Bella Coola hospital still covered in dirt. The hospital staff were afraid to clean him or move him, for fear of damaging him further. Eventually, he was flown to Vancouver where he stayed for several months while recuperating.

Dave's horrible injury was a valuable lesson for all of us. We knew that we better take heed if we were going to survive in this new land.

It was several weeks before we settled down and became our old selves again. We knew things were getting back to normal when we started calling Dave "Potato Nose" and we returned to our busy schedules that we enjoyed so much.

3

CULTURE SHOCK

Changing weather patterns over a vast area greatly influenced the sporadic behavior of the Bella Coola River. The river often behaved like a woman with a temperamental disposition, and her mood was never predictable. For those who drifted her course regularly while fishing, it was common knowledge that the lady could change her mind every day. At times, she even changed her course.

Averaging one hundred feet across and ten feet deep, the lady usually moved along at eight miles per hour. In the spring and fall, however, when she became unruly, she gorged herself on side-valley tributaries. The increased volume of water produced a much swifter pace for the lady. The streams she fed on were often referred to as creeks, but in California, we would have recognized them as fair-sized rivers. The effect of these so called "creeks" constantly created a fluctuation in depth--as much as twelve feet in some areas.

A main tributary that greatly influenced the lady's disposition was the Talchako. It acted as a funnel and drain for a glacier two miles wide, two hundred feet tall, and fifty miles long.

Another factor was the Atnarko. Its source was melting snow in the higher elevations around

Turner and Lonesome Lakes. When the clear snow waters of the Atnarko joined together with the milky glacier waters of the Talchako, their confluence became the headwaters of the Bella Coola River.

Run-off from the 9500 foot Mount Noosatsum combined both snow and glacier water to form the Noosatsum River. With several high peaks dominating the landscape of the Bella Coola Valley, other streams were formed such as the Klonnick, Thorsen, Fish, Snootli, Saloompt, and Noosgulch. Eventually, each one met up with the lady.

Once, while trying to divert the Bella Coola River, the road crew strung a cable across her expanse, with huge logs attached. Later, when the lady reached her crest, the crew heard the cable singing in a high-pitched tone as it became tight like a violin string. The steel line, two inches in diameter, had a two-hundred-ton rating, but it didn't take long to snap. The lady proved just how powerful and uncompromising she could be.

With such a powerful influence ruling the Valley, the river became the focus of many conversations. This was especially true at the local hangout, Wilf Nygaard's Sporting Good's Store. The hangout was located between Hagensborg and the Bella Coola townsite. It not only supplied hardware, tools, rifles, fishing rods, reels, lures, and hipwaders, but it also provided a meeting place for what locals referred to as 'the hot stove club'. On any given day, club members could receive priceless fishing tips from experienced sportsmen, along with information on the latest river conditions.

When tourists stopped at the local meeting place, they too could receive valuable information on the best fishing gear to use, river conditions, safety tips, and any problem bears along the river. All they had to do was ask. If they didn't ask, then no information was offered.

When a group of visiting fishermen lost all their equipment and gear in a well-known whirlpool and log jam while drifting the Bella Coola River, they quickly asked why no one warned them about the hazard.

They were promptly informed, "You didn't ask."

On another occasion, a tourist told the hot stove members he had a solution for bear problems: "Just leave them alone and they'll leave you alone."

Sometime later, seasoned club members were drifting the upper river. They noticed that same fisherman swimming like mad down the river, just to get away from a huge grizzly. The bear had taken all his freshly caught fish. Hot stove members were treated to a great story that evening.

There was another club, of sorts, that people often referred to as the 'old-timers'. In an isolated land of limited sunlight, folks always seemed a little pale, but the ashen tones of this particular group reflected their sentiment toward variety or change. For them, a common diet was cooked mush in the morning and boiled fish with potatoes in the evening--seven days a week!

What the old-timers lacked in diversity, they made up for it in ingenuity, industry, hard work, love of the simple life, honesty, and family values. Old-timers had managed to eke out an existence where most would have failed, and it had been by the sweat of their brows, and many years of hard work. Most of them had never received a formal education, or experienced such things as television, a stop light, painted lines down a road, a three-story building, pizza, a barbershop, a phone booth, or a dental office. But I soon recognized that these self-sustaining people had their own kind of enlightenment, and little by little, I came to appreciate them for what they really were. A special breed.

With this in mind, I decided it was time to branch out, so I invited a couple of old-timers over for dinner. Gary and Sandy were away for the evening and I thought it would be a good time to get acquainted.

Manly and Dora (not their real names) arrived for dinner. I decided to use my best dishes, called Franciscan Ware, hauled clear across the Chilcotin all the way from California. The dishes had a bright red apple and green leaf design, a very popular print in the States.

I wanted to make a good impression and prepare a meal I could be proud of, so I prepared spaghetti, one of our favorites. I reminded myself to serve our visitors first.

When Manly and Dora sat down to eat with us, Manly immediately tensed up. I asked if I could serve him, but he didn't even acknowledge my offer.

"Why don't you just serve yourself," I offered, trying to appease him.

Dave didn't have any problem serving himself, so he dished up a plate, but Manly and Dora didn't budge. I sensed something was amiss.

"Is something wrong?" I asked.

"Oh, nothing really," Dora said, her face glowing with redness. Manly continued his tense posture and didn't blink an eye.

Then Dora said, "I'm a little embarrassed."

"What is it?" I asked.

"It's the plate," Dora said sheepishly. "Manly can't eat on a plate like that, eh?"

"Oh no, is it dirty?" I asked, horrified. I felt my face turn red too.

"No, it's not dirty...it's the design. Manly can't eat on a plate like that, he doesn't like the apples and the bright colors."

"Oh," I said with relief. "Let me get something else."

I found a plain white plate in the cupboard that I thought might do, and placed it before Manly. But he still didn't move or say a word. Then I realized that Manly hadn't spoken a word since he sat down. Dora had acted as his interpreter, and somehow, she knew what he was thinking. I was fascinated with this concept, and quickly shot a glance at the interpreter for an explanation.

"I'm so embarrassed," Dora said. "Manly won't eat the spaghetti."

"Why?" I asked.

"Manly has never eaten spaghetti."

Silence filled the room and I looked over at Manly who resembled a petrified tree in an ancient forest.

I directed my question to the interpreter. "But wouldn't he like to try it?"

"No, I think not. Manly can really be stubborn when it comes to things like this, eh?"

By then, Dave was finishing his first serving and was about to reach for another. He didn't seem too concerned about the bright design, or for that matter, the strange ventriloquist act taking place at the table. I didn't know what to say, so I tried to be accommodating.

"Well...can I fix something else...for Manly?" I said, stumbling on each word as it fell out of my mouth.

"Don't worry about it," Dora said, standing up. "I'll just take him home and fix him something to eat. He likes meat and potatoes, and that's about all he will eat. I guess I should have mentioned that to you, eh?"

I felt sorry for Dora so I tried to smooth things over.

The couple walked toward the door and Dora apologized once more. Manly still hadn't spoken or changed the blank expression on his traumatized face.

"What was that all about?" Dave asked after they left.

"Well," I said, rubbing my chin, "I think Manly *might* be just a little set in his ways."

The evening had been a disaster, and somewhere in the back of my mind, I felt my reputation as a homemaker was on the line.

It was during this time I learned about a strange phenomena that occurs when people live in a small fish bowl community where everyone knows each other's activities and business. The phenomena is this: You end up doing strange things that you normally wouldn't think of doing. These actions are directly linked to the knowledge that no matter what you do, someone will think it odd and talk about it to someone else. And, because of this, one finds strange things to do just to substantiate what they think is being said. I'm not sure if this theory can be found in books on human behavior. If not, it should be. I offer the following story to prove my point.

One night, at a church dinner, the planned entertainment didn't show up. Trying to make do, someone volunteered me to sing for everyone. The well-meaning announcer just assumed that because I came from a musically talented family, I too had been so blessed. But nothing could be further from the truth. I can hardly carry a tune!

Trying to appease the announcer, and live up to what was expected, I walked to the center stage. Looking out at the audience, the phenomena took over, and I began singing the only song I knew all the words to--off key.

Does your chewing gum loose its flavor
On the bedpost over night?
If your Mama says don't chew it
Do you swallow it in spite?
And you catch it on your tonsils
And you heave it left and right.
Does your chewing gum lose its flavor
On the bedpost over night.

I sang several verses before I realized it was the phenomenon at work. Fortunately, no one ever asked me to sing again.

I learned that part of the Bella Coola set-ways was not to give up on a garment just because it was out of style or showed a little wear, and I'm sure some of those garments had been products of the early 1900's. Style wasn't a concern for those with set-ways, and because of this, commodities seemed to have a "millennial shelf life" at the local Co-op. If a garment served a practical purpose, then it didn't have to be fashionable. Style just wasn't in the Bella Coola dictionary of life. Bella Coola had developed a set-style all its own.

Local women wore gumboots while outdoors and it didn't matter if it was shopping day, church day, or visiting day. It was the accepted set-way Bella Coola footwear. Any type of coat was acceptable, even if it was 20-years-old, as long as it was warm.

What women lacked in style, they made up for in elegant homemaking skills. They served their food in a stylish manner on hand-crocheted tablecloths with beautiful china that had been handed down from one generation to another, usually in the form of a dowry. Each homemaker collected beautiful individual cup and saucer patterns of quality china. These collections were usually displayed with pride, and it didn't matter if it was on a plywood shelf or a hand-crafted buffet from the old country.

Bella Coola women were truly masters of the needle crafts. A number of them still used the old treadle sewing machines, perhaps just as well if not more skillfully than their mothers and grandmothers before them. They all knitted baby sweaters and booties, crocheted tablecloths, dresses, and doilies, and embroidered beautiful tablecloths and pillowcases. When at rest, their hands were never idle. There was no problem with millennial shelf life when it came to craft threads at the Co-op. They rotated quite regularly on their own, and it was difficult to keep them in stock.

The men all worked in logging, or some form of outdoor activity, so their clothing was standard: GWG pants with red pocket loop, flannel shirt, dark green goose-down vest covered with grease on the front, heavy calked boots, and a red hard hat. Dave refused to wear the GWG pants, with their wide pant leg, so he ordered Levis from the States. Of course everyone noticed them, they'd never seen Levis before.

A man's vehicle seemed to reflect a certain kind of status, and it was either a GMC or a Ford pickup. Status meant everything to the men folk. New trucks were very rare, so the way a man maintained his vehicle seemed to tell more about his status than anything else. If his truck ran good, and looked good, it didn't matter if it was old, he still had status. If his vehicle didn't run well, had dents in the body, or a broken headlight, then he didn't have status. There were two exceptions that didn't effect status. Everyone had a cracked windshield, due to the many rocks being flipped up by logging trucks, and it was normal to have mud and dirt on a vehicle.

Socials were for everyone. It didn't matter if it was a dance, a dinner, or a picnic. Children often listened to the same music as their parents and danced the same dances. The big event of the year was the Fall Fair, in September, and everyone in the Valley took part. I wrote home about this big event:

Dear Folks,

Boy, have we been busy! Last Friday was the beginning of Fall Fair. There was a western dance in the evening and we really had a good time. The next day was the logger's competitions. They were really something to see. Ruth's brother, Cliff Nygaard, won most of the events, including the pole climbing contest. Using spurs and a rope, he went to the top of a 100 foot pole, rang the bell, and made it back down in 35 seconds. The log-rolling event was great too, because the spectators as well as the competitors got wet.

There were so many booths with wonderful displays of needle crafts, garden produce, flowers, homemade desserts, and canned items. I've never seen so much homemade stuff in all my life!

Yesterday there was a big picnic. All the men went fishing for trout and brought back 170 of them. We fried and fried fish. There were all kinds of salads and desserts to go with the meal. Later, we played croquet, basketball, horseshoes, and baseball.

We sure don't miss television. There is so much visiting going on all the time, it kind of fills the void. If we don't go visiting ourselves, then we have to be prepared for company, and that includes serving a homemade dessert.

Take care, Carolyn

Everything about our new life was exciting to me and I tried to keep my family posted on our acclimation to the Valley.

I couldn't help noticing how easily Johnny seemed to roll with the waves of adaptation, kind of like a sailboat moving along in a soft breeze. Barbara Gurr might have had something to do with that. After all, Johnny had shown an interest in her right from the beginning.

When school started in September, Johnny attended Sir Alexander Mackensie High School in Hagensborg. Being a good-looking foreigner and having musical abilities put Johnny in good stead with the local girls. Shortly after his arrival, after the news spread about a new young man living in the Crown Zellerbach house, twelve local girls, his age, rode up on bicycles. They started singing: "We love you Johnny, oh yes we do."

Johnny was a little embarrassed, but he soon got used to all the attention. I thought he might get an over-sized head but relaxed a little when I heard him talking to the Gurr boys.

"Why don't you boys come over for some croquet later, and...oh yeah...why don't you bring your sister Barbara along."

Johnny found the Canadian academic system more difficult than California's. He was used to little effort and lots of socializing, but still managed a B-average. In his new school, he was expected to work and this took some getting used to. Johnny's socializing experience did pay off though, when he was elected class president, then school vice president during his first year at Sir Alexander Mackensie High School.

Some of his high school teachers were good, and some weren't so good. One teacher was so strict, there was only one place to write your name on a piece of paper: "Exactly 1/2 inch from the top of the page, and be sure to measure with your ruler and draw a line."

One time this same teacher was explaining how a battery works, but Johnny was sure she was saying it all wrong. He quickly raised his hand and pointed this out to her and the class. The teacher suddenly became very upset. In a snippety tone, she asked if Johnny wanted to teach the class. When he said "yes," and started for the front of the room, the teacher screamed at the top of her lungs, "Sit down!"

Johnny formed a rock and roll band called the Contours and Gary became the manger for the group. Playing at dances in the wild Anahim Lake area proved to be very interesting. Dances

56

seemed to bring out the worst of the worst in that country and consequently, upright citizens felt safer staying at home. Every dance seemed to turn into a brawl with lots of serious fighting taking place.

Just before one dance, a Native man had killed another Native, then fled into the back country with the Mounties in hot pursuit. The killer and his victim each had brothers who showed up at the Contour's dance. Right away, the two men got into a serious fight. One ended up laying on the dance floor while the other proceeded to kick him in the face. People tried to break it up but the kicker pulled out a knife. Finally, the band members joined together and were able to turn the guy around, pushing him outside. They quickly closed the door and stationed a very large Native man to keep it closed. Then the dance continued.

Each hall in the Bella Coola Valley seemed to produce a new and distinct catastrophe while Johnny continued to play his rock and roll rhythms. At Lobelco hall, one dance degenerated into a twelve person brawl. Johnny was playing on stage one minute, then seconds later, he was flat on the floor crammed into a coat room at the other end of the hall. Sitting on top of him was a very large Native boy.

While playing at the Nuxalk Hall, Johnny kept a watchful eye on two suspicious characters who were sipping alcoholic beverages off stage. The hall was suppose to be a dry hall. When the Mounties arrived and tried to apprehend the law breakers, everyone got into the act, including the band. The highlight of the evening was a big wrestling match in the middle of the dance floor.

At the Moose Hall, Johnny was performing on stage when he noticed a guy slap his dancing partner hard enough to knock her down. Although it was none of his business, Johnny quickly slipped off his electric guitar, leaped from the stage, and wrestled the man to the floor.

The Contours traveled to Bella Bella, a Native fishing village fifty miles west of Bella Coola. While there, Johnny had to get permission from the local chief just to spend the night. No one appeared to anxious to have him in their village.

It didn't take Johnny long to realize that these Native people felt they had been dealt a terrible hand in history, and it was very obvious they had a great deal of animosity towards the white man. It was on this same trip that Johnny experienced wild duck stew and fresh salmon row dried on cedar boughs.

When Johnny wasn't playing for the Contours, he was out hustling work to earn money for band equipment. One job he landed was working at the Namu fish cannery near the mouth of the Burke Channel Inlet.

Upon his arrival at the cannery, Johnny concluded the Native word for Namu meant "big stink" due to the horribly-foul fish stench that contaminated the air for miles around. He soon learned that the smell contaminated work clothes to such an extent, that in time, they had to be destroyed.

During salmon season, a person could pull down big money at the cannery while working all kinds of overtime. Johnny learned that one fellow, anxious to increase his earnings, had worked a 96-hour shift. This was just the type of job he was looking for.

In order to work at the cannery, Johnny had to lie about his age and say that he was sixteen, instead of fourteen-years-old. At first, he was stuck in the dark hull of a fishing boat with three other shadows, given a gaff, and told to fill a loading net with fish. It sounded simple, but trying with all his might, he couldn't get one fish in the net. For the Natives working with him, it was simple. They speared the fish with ease, flipped them in the net, and continued right on. After struggling to get the hang of fish spearing, Johnny decided to relocate himself to another part of the plant. No one ever seemed to notice, or care.

Unknowingly, the place he promoted himself to was the dreaded fertilizer factory. Anyone working there had to change clothes each day before eating at the mess hall, or everyone complained.

At the fertilizer factory, decaying fish were dumped in large cement rooms with vats that had long troughs and rotating augers, processing fish into a putrid mush. Later, the mush was allowed to dry after being transported by pipe to another area. One of the most dreaded jobs was dealing with line breaks that sent fetid goo spilling out all over. But the worst job of all was climbing into the vats when they were almost empty, and shoveling out the remaining fish-slime into the auger-trough. By then, the pungent vapors were more like ether, and were so strong, one fellow fainted. Unfortunately, he landed face down in the fish-slime.

Having his fill of the fertilizer factory, Johnny relocated himself again. This time he went to the canning line where the fish were gutted, trimmed, flayed, de-boned, and canned. Johnny's job was to line each fish up so its head could be sliced off by a mechanical blade. He thought he finally had it made. Then he noticed a co-worker with an ugly scar across his hand the exact shape of the cutting blade.

On to another job in the assembly line where fish had to be sorted by type: king, hump, pink, sockeye; better yet, pink eye, dogthroat, and coyote. Johnny couldn't tell the difference.

When he'd earned enough money for his Fender twin reverb guitar amp, Johnny gladly quit the cannery business and headed for home. As far as he was concerned, it was not a moment too soon.

Sometime later, while needing more money, Johnny landed a part time job in Ocean Falls, sixty miles west of Bella Coola. Like most ports in the inlet, it too was an isolated community with steep rugged mountains, and was accessible only by air or sea. But Ocean Falls had a pulp mill, and it was larger than most coastal fishing villages. It also had a paved road and the Bella Coola Road Department was responsible for maintaining it. So, when Mack Gurr sent a road crew to Ocean Falls, Johnny landed a job clearing brush.

Johnny quickly concluded Ocean Falls was the Native word for "rain," because it fell in ocean proportions--two hundred inches a year. He determined this while standing in a wet ditch along the wet road in a wet slicker using a wet machete to slap the wet brush that sprayed his wet face every time he hacked at it.

When Johnny returned from his soggy ordeal, Mack had a nice, quiet, dry job for him in the Valley. Mack needed someone to stay at his house for a few days while he and his family were out of the Valley on a trip.

"Not bad," Johnny thought.

So he moved into the Gurr home and stayed for ten days. On the last day of his house-sitting, a magazine salesman knocked on the door and before he left, Johnny had signed up for $25 worth of magazine subscriptions. The salesman only needed a few more sales to win a trip to Hawaii. How could Johnny refuse that?

About the time Johnny came to his senses and realized that magazines weren't on his "must have" list, a couple of friends stopped by. They quickly noticed the perplexed look on Johnny's face. Johnny didn't want to tell them what he'd done because he was feeling just a little bit stupid. Intrigued by the mystery, the two friends decided to lock Johnny out of the house until he gave up his big secret.

Johnny knew where the Gurr's secret key was hidden outside, so he soon re-entered the house and ran down a hall toward the bathroom, with his friends in hot pursuit. They almost caught him, but Johnny quickly jumped into the bathroom, then slammed the door on them. The two boys pushed against the door as hard as they could. Then, BANG! Everyone froze. The door had been ripped loose from its hinges.

The Gurrs were due back in the morning and there stood Johnny with their bathroom door in his hands. Shocked, he looked at his friends. They looked at him. Then, the boys turned and made a fast exit with an over the shoulder "see you later."

Several hours later, after many failed attempts, Johnny was able, with the aid of toothpicks and carpenter's glue, to get the door more or less hung and working.

It was weeks later when one of the Gurr boys got in big trouble for leaning against the bathroom door and knocking it loose from the hinges. Lucky for Johnny, no one noticed the toothpicks.

But, fate has a way of punishing those who deceive.

Sometime later, Johnny attended a teenage party at Lily Gorden's house. Feeling hungry, he looked around the kitchen for something to eat and found a table loaded with food. Right away, he spotted his favorite dessert, chocolate chip cookies. And boy were they big! Quickly, he crammed a whole cookie in his mouth.

No one had mentioned they only looked like cookies, but were really Norwegian fish cakes, a must at any party. Somehow, the flavor of fish when expecting chocolate, seemed to arouse dormant memories of the fish fertilizer plant at Bella Bella. Turning pale at the thought of fish-slime, Johnny quickly ran for an exit. Opening the door, he was just in time to welcome party guests with a preview of the evening's meal.

4

The Old Homestead

Before our trip north, friends in California joked with us about what to expect for mail delivery service in the isolated community of Bella Coola.

"They probably make a dog-sled run every ten days or so," one friend had commented.

A dog-sled probably would have been more reliable. As it was, we depended on a float plane with mail service from Vancouver each Saturday. The inlet provided an excellent landing surface if good weather conditions prevailed. All too often, during winter storms, air travel was completely halted. At times, we felt fortunate to receive mail twice a month.

Every Thursday, a large ship from Vancouver docked at the wharf to deliver supplies of fresh food, plus any individual orders that had been placed with the "Simpson-Sears" catalog. Because this was the only day fresh milk and produce could be purchased, everyone traveled to the townsite on that day. Shopping excursions always turned into mini-reunions with friends and relatives all meeting in one area: the Bella Coola Co-op.

The Co-op was a small, busy building that housed everything from food items to fabric and hardware. It was difficult at best to concentrate on shopping needs because of all the visiting going on. People visited everywhere, all the way from the meat counter to the ax and shovel aisle. Wandering through narrow aisles with old hard-to-push carts made it even more difficult.

The Co-op operated a lunch counter and it was the only place in town to purchase prepared food. We never ate at the counter because we couldn't afford it. Food items cost three times what we were used to paying in the States and in some cases, five times as much. The lunch counter food, with its added fees, was just too expensive. Consequently, all of our meals were eaten at home or at someone's house as an invited guest where, most often, wild game or fresh fish was served. There was also luscious homemade rolls, baked beans, home-canned vegetables, and homemade desserts.

Our relatives and new-found friends were so generous with gifts of wild game and fish delivered to our door, plus dinner invitations, we didn't even miss eating out at restaurants.

Food cravings plagued me constantly because I was pregnant. As a result, I usually had a special longing in mind when I visited the Co-op. The candy aisle produced a very poor selection, not to mention the fact I didn't recognize any of the brand names. Craving M&M's, Bridge Mix or a Baby Ruth candy bar was futile. The Co-op had never shelved such delicacies. As a food-craving pregnant woman on a low budget, I was very much aware of the poor selection, limited quantities and high prices.

To solve my sweet cravings, I focused on the one thing that I found, recognized and could afford. It was the one-cent gum-ball machine located at the entrance of the Co-op. Because I didn't want anyone to see me placing fifty pennies (a week's supply) into the machine, it was necessary to persuade four-year-old Clint to do the task for me. The only problem was, he wouldn't settle for anything less than a fifty-fifty split. His sweet tooth was every bit as big as mine.

It was a common practice to purchase some items at the Hagensborg Store on Thursday during the return journey up the Valley. The first time I stopped at the store, I was amazed to find strange wooden slats hanging on an outside wall. Soon, a logger, on his way home from work, walked over and grabbed two slats. He bent over and attached each slat to the bottom of his calked boots. This provided a shield for the flooring inside the store from the metal spikes on the boots. The slats were referred to as boot sandals. Inside the store, the plodding sound created by large men in strange footwear provided a unique audible rhythm that I would forever associate with that place of business.

There was another strange thing that caught my eye at the Hagensborg store. Backwoods people, who had traveled long distances by foot or by horse, sometimes showed up there to purchase the necessities. These backward human beings, used to living alone and away from civilization, were so bushed they usually didn't speak to anyone. Very often, they hid themselves behind food isles so they wouldn't be noticed at all.

On one particular Thursday shopping trip to the townsite, Ruth and I traveled together in her car. As she drove along, I explained to Ruth how difficult it was to find a place for Dave and I to rent. Nothing was available in the Valley. We knew that eventually, other family members living in California, would be making the long trek north to Bella Coola. We definitely needed another house.

Ruth and I passed by a large two-story house that lay just beyond Snootli Creek, in an area known as the Snootli Stretch. Ruth pointed out that Andy Widsten had come into the Valley, by way of his tugboat, and was staying at his family's old homestead. Andy currently lived in Shearwater, a fishing village 100 miles west of Bella Coola. Ruth went on to explain that Andy purchased wood products from the local Northcop Sawmill and barged them to various construction and building sites in the inlet. At that time, Northcop Sawmill was the only operating mill in a two hundred mile radius. Andy was kept very busy while supplying the valuable wood products to various ports with such items as large beams and construction grade fir and cedar. With Andy away so much, Ruth thought that perhaps the old homestead might be available to rent.

"Perhaps Andy Widsten will rent to you, eh?" Ruth said.

"Let's stop on the way back from town," I replied, feeling somewhat encouraged.

Normally shop-visit day (as I called it) took about three hours. I'd never shopped with Ruth before. On this particular day, after five hours in town and much visiting, I became aware that Ruth was related to everyone in the Valley. She was one of thirteen children. Her mother, Camilla Saugstad Nygaard, was the daughter of Reverend Christian Saugstad, the original Norwegian settler back in 1895. The culture of these fair-skinned people had remained captured in the Valley, the result of years of isolation from outside influences.

To say that Ruth came from good, moral, pioneer stock thriving on industry would be an under-statement. Her life had been formed and nurtured by a group of idealistic, God-fearing people originating from a common homeland. Her wholesome, homespun character reflected the teachings of the old country values. She was truly the sweetest, most sincere person I have ever met.

The old country influence formed by early pioneers, along with the original inhabitants, the Nuxalk Native people, blended into a unique duo-cultural ambiance.

Two large totem poles announced the entrance to the Bella Coola Native village and symbolized a people of great cultural history. At one time, thousands of Nuxalk people had lived in the coastal area, in as many as 103 villages.

Their history told of great hunters, fishermen and traders. They used fishing nets to capture the ooligans that spawned by the thousands in the mouth of the river. The small herring-like fish were rendered down, and the grease that was produced, was used for trading purposes with tribes from the outer coast and the interior. The routes used by the Nuxalk to the interior tribes became known as the Grease Trails.

Upon each visit to the townsite, I drank in the unique atmosphere and marveled at the two distinct cultural groups. I also noticed an identifiable Canadian influence in the expression "eh" that was used by all. The word served as a common speech denominator for both cultures.

"You're going to town, eh?" "You're feeling well, eh?" "The food was great, eh?"

How I loved listening to this new lingo.

Another colloquialism was their short-vowel sounds compared to our American long-vowel sounds. Our t-r-o-u-t became troot, a-b-o-u-t became aboot, and g-a-r-a-g-e became grage. On the other hand, the long "e" sound was over-emphasized in words like reeely and beeen. I found this all quite amusing.

Most interesting of all was a strange sound I'd never heard before. In the Norwegian dialect there was a soft sounding "Yu" that was expressed almost in a whisper. It was made by sucking air into the throat quickly but cutting it off sharply, almost like a hiccup. The expression was used as a response to the affirmative. "You're going to town, eh?" The whispered response, "Yu."

Their impression of our California dialect was often revealed by a sudden burst of laughter, and we would be left in ignorance as to the source of their amusement. Often times, I was asked to repeat a word that brought many a laugh to Norwegian faces. It was c-o-w-b-o-y, with emphasis on long-vowel sounds and speaking like I had a southern accent.

The real differential between us was speed. Speed in the way we talked and moved. Being from California, talking and moving quickly was second nature. I was often asked to repeat a lengthy dissertation after being told to slow down and speak more clearly.

Our appearance reflected professional hair cuts (Sandy was a cosmetologist) and well-maintained teeth by a California dentist. By contrast, untrained barbers performed hair cuts on their own family members and the closest dentist was 300 miles away. Home-cut hair do's sometimes took on strange appearances and it was common to see missing teeth when someone smiled. I was told that the only difference in a bad hair cut and a good hair cut is "two weeks" and people don't need "so many" teeth anyway.

On that Thursday afternoon, exhausted from hours of visiting and shopping, Ruth and I headed back up the Valley toward the Snootli Stretch and Andy Widsten's house. I could only hope he was still there and that possibly, he would rent his house to me.

We pulled into the driveway on the west side of the house. Andy Widsten stood close by talking to a strange-looking fellow named Ted Brooks. Ted had a long white beard and except for the constant scowl on his face, he resembled Santa Claus.

"Hi," I said, as I approached the two men.

Both men nodded but seemed to be dumb-founded as to who I might be. They continued their stare then glanced toward the car to see if it would offer any clues as to my identity.

"I'm Caroline Foltzed. I wonder if your house is for rent?"

Both men stood in place with an apprehensive stare.

Finally Andy replied, "No, I'm not renting this house."

"Are you sure?" I tried to display my best available smile and sincere look.

"Where are you from?" Andy asked.

"California. My husband works for Crown Zellerbach."

This didn't seem to enlighten or impress either one them. After a short pause, I added, "I'm Lige Gurr's niece."

Well, this seemed to make a difference. The two men changed their posture and appeared to relax a little. Using Lige Gurr's name to anyone in the Valley was like handing them a resume with references of the greatest kind. His name and reputation was as good as gold.

"Well...I have been thinking about doing something with this old place. Maybe I can show it to you."

We started toward the huge, two-story structure with its old-fashioned porch running the full length across the back of the house. Looking over my shoulder, I could see that Ted Brooks walked in the opposite direction from us. He was heading toward a large meadow that lay between Andy's house and a small log cabin nestled back in a stand of cedars.

Later, I would learn that the Australian-born Ted Brooks did not like women at all, and considered himself a hermit. He had been the caretaker of the Widsten homestead for many years while Andy conducted his business out at Shearwater.

Andy and I entered the house through the kitchen door. Suddenly, I became aware of the character and charm of the old place. It was a case of love at first sight.

The kitchen was designed for a big family. It had an oil stove on one side with a large cupboard adjacent. Across the room was an oak, claw-foot dining room table with eight matching oak chairs. Next to the door that we had entered, was a second table, painted white, with matching chairs. On the wall closest to the porch was a small wooden door. Upon opening it, I could see that it was an icebox. It was a simple, but effective, wooden box attached to the outside wall of the house.

Andy explained that he'd grown up in the house and was the eldest of twelve children raised there. His father had been killed while Andy was still young, in a logging accident. As the oldest child, Andy had learned at an early age to work and provide for the large family.

Twelve children? No wonder the kitchen seemed so large.

Above the stove was a strange apparatus made of wood that measured three by five feet. It had several wooden slats and was suspended in air by a rope attached to pulleys.

"What is that?" I asked.

Andy slowly lowered the device to about shoulder level. "Clothes rack for drying," he said. "The rising heat from the stove dries clothes real fast, eh?"

I could see metal grates in the ceiling. I pointed at them with a bewildered stare.

"The rising heat from the stove goes into the upstairs bedrooms, eh?" Andy replied.

"I'll be darned," I said using my long vowel-sounding American accent.

Andy smiled.

Next, he showed me a room that had once been a bedroom, that was converted into a bathroom, only a few years earlier when indoor plumbing was installed. It was the largest bathroom I've ever seen--12 by 15 feet. A white porcelain claw-footed bathtub, eight feet long, sat next to the wall.

A closet door was opened and there on the wall, mounted horizontally, was a hot water tank. Andy explained that the water-coils inside the kitchen stove heated and exchanged water, while circulating it through the hot water tank.

I then realized the oil stove in the kitchen not only heated the downstairs area, but the upstairs as well, dried clothes, cooked food and heated household water. The stove was the hub of a very efficient heat exchange.

We then walked through a bedroom that was off the kitchen and from there we entered the living room. Andy explained the bedroom had once been a dining room.

I looked out over the living room. It reminded me of what I would call a parlor. It had a red-to-mauve tapestry type rug, and furniture and lamps that looked like something from the 1930's. A cast iron stove sat to one side. In one corner, I could see an old-fashioned treadle sewing machine.

Andy opened a door exposing a stairwell. We walked up the stairs.

"When was this house built?" I asked.

"About 1900. It was made from clear Valley fir, the best, eh?"

The four upstairs bedrooms were furnished in old bed-frames, antique mirrors, and even a baby crib. The more I saw of the house, the more I wanted to rent it. My adoration of the house must have shone through as it became apparent to the owner.

Andy and I squared off in the upstairs hallway.

"Do you think you might rent it to me?" I asked holding my breath.

Andy paused for a minute. He scratched his head, deep in thought.

"Actually, I've been thinking about selling this old house, eh?" he said.

"You have?" I couldn't believe what I was hearing.

"Yu," came the Norwegian expression to the affirmative.

"What do you think you would want for it?" Again, I held my breath.

Andy took a long pause. "$1,200."

My mouth fell open. How could this be?

In my dazed non-believing state, I asked if he would sell any furnishings with the house.

He responded by saying he already had all his personal belongings moved out, so he would be willing to sell the rest of the furniture.

"Two hundred dollars total, for the furniture, eh?"

Again I was amazed.

"There is one small thing, one small detail," he said.

"What?" I asked, ready to promise the moon.

"I want the house moved, eh?"

It took a moment for this to sink in then I began to contemplate just what he was inferring. I figured the house had about 3,000 square feet, plus two very large front and back porches.

"Is that possible?" I asked.

"I think so," Andy replied.

I looked down at the hardwood floor.

Andy continued, "I want to build a new house on the same foundation, eh?"

"Where would I move it to?" I asked, feeling like we were making up a story as we went along.

"Well, I have five acres on the opposite side of the road. I'll sell it to you."

My eyebrows went up. Andy caught the meaning of this gesture.

"Two hundred and fifty dollars an acre," he responded.

I was dumb-founded. I wondered if this was the deal of the century or an impossible feat. I didn't have the vaguest idea how to go about moving a house, especially a very large house.

Andy continued. "There is someone in the Valley who has moved structures before, at logging camps, eh? His name is Elmer Sollid and he lives next to the Hagensborg Store. His wife, Christine, works at the post office in the store.

I didn't know Elmer but an image of Christine's face flashed before me. I had spoken to her on many different occasions. She was a very nice lady who sorted mail for the residents living in the upper Valley.

"I know Christine," I offered, deep in thought.

"Elmer can help you, eh?" Andy reiterated.

"OK..." I replied slowly. "It sounds good to me. Do you want to draw up papers on all this so my husband and I can sign them?"

Andy stretched out his hand and said, "As far as I'm concerned, if we shake hands on it, then we have a deal, eh?"

Andy shook my trembling hand, establishing our agreement.

Moments later, I walked slowly toward Ruth's car. My mind was still reeling from the conversation and agreement with Andy. I glanced toward the massive structure that now appeared ten times larger than it had before. My face was frozen in a blank, expressionless stare as I climbed into the car.

"He rented it to you, eh?" Ruth inquired.

I shook my head implying no. Then I said, "He sold it to me."

"He sold it to you, eh?" Ruth's face took on a surprised look as her eyebrows leaped upward.

I stared out the car window at the enormous house, trying to envision moving something that big, that weighed so much.

"He sold it to you, eh?" Ruth repeated.

In my mind-boggled state, all I could do was suck in air and respond, "Yu."

5

Snootli Stretch Moving Day

The Bella Coola Valley is approximately 40 miles long from the base of the hill to the townsite. In 1965, power lines ran from the townsite and continued up the valley as far as Sy Nystrom's place, approximately 18 miles.

Anyone living beyond Sy's place either had a gas-powered generator or used the old methods of living. Many families still used kerosene lamps to light their darkened rooms at night in the Firvale and Stuie areas in the upper Valley.

Asphalt pavement was considered one of God's greatest gifts for those living next to the only route through the valley. It provided a welcome relief from the endless dust-clouds of passing motorists. The pavement extended from the townsite to a few miles beyond Hagensborg for a total of 15 miles. The Snootli Stretch lay right in between.

To me, property eight miles from the townsite, on a paved road with electricity, had all the appeal of a gold mine and was something well worth pursuing. Even the price seemed reasonable. I had returned from the Snootli Stretch that day knowing that I'd found my new home. All I had to do was convince Dave. I could only imagine what his reaction would be when I broke the news about the gigantic house that I'd committed to purchase; plus, "Oh, by the way, you'll have to move it across the road to five acres that I also committed to buy."

This wasn't going to be easy. I expected a big reaction, and Dave didn't disappoint me. It took a couple of days for him to settle down after a quick drive-by to inspect the structure he was required to move. His first reaction: "Totally impossible. A house that size cannot be moved. You've got to be kidding. I don't know anything about moving a house!"

Dave continued to give me dirty looks and shake his head every time he looked at me. Plus, he kept mumbling to himself, words I could never quite make out. This went on for several days.

In the meantime, we experienced a series of events that suddenly took precedence over the proposed purchase of the Widsten house.

The weather turned cold. Snow started falling earlier than normal and continued to fall until the high country reached great depths. Then, the worst thing that could happen, under those conditions, did happen. A Chinook wind started blowing, and the warming trend transformed snow into rain.

Streams in the high country swelled as melting snow filled them to capacity. They soon became raging torrents as they gravitated downward to lower levels. The Bella Coola River bulged with the gushing water, and soon became a raging force that tore away and eroded river banks at will. The river banks gave way to falling trees that became giant ramming forces, assaulting anything in their way. Most of the bridges providing access to inhabited areas of the valley were reduced to piles of rubble.

When the river had swelled as high as a person thought possible, it swelled even more. The high water was nothing new to the old-timers, but to us, it looked as if the whole valley was going to erode and wash away.

The Crown Zellerbach house sat high on its foundation and was a quarter mile from the river. I will never forget the sick feeling in my stomach when I looked out the kitchen window and saw the Bella Coola River in our back yard.

As news spread by what is known as the "moccasin telegraph," we learned the extent of the damage.

In the upper Valley, Keith Mecham, 15-year-old son of Floyd and Inez Mecham, had almost been swept away in raging water when a bridge collapsed. The cattle truck he was driving was completely destroyed.

Almost every bridge had been taken out by high water carrying large trees. In some of the outlying areas, adjacent to the Bella Coola River, several families had been hemmed in by high water.

Homes in the lower part of the Valley, close to the townsite, were hardest hit. They not only had to deal with the high river water, but were also subject to incoming tides from the Burke Channel Inlet. As a result, many people were left homeless.

Residents living in the Saloompt Valley, on the north side of the Bella Coola River, were cut off from all stores and supplies. The Saloompt Bridge had been one of the largest in the Valley, sitting high off the water. I couldn't believe it was gone.

Finally, the water started to subside, and we witnessed how quickly a small community can pull together in time of need. Ferries were set up to relay supplies of milk and food to stranded families, while others housed and fed the homeless.

A letter written to my parents in California read:

Dear Folks,

I'm sure you'll have heard about our flood by the time this letter reaches you. It was the worst, according to the old-timers, since 1936. There was sure a lot of damage, especially to bridges.

Do you remember Floyd and Inez Mecham? They live in the upper part of the valley. They lost their son Barry just a short time ago in a logging accident, and almost lost their second son, Keith, during the flood. Keith was crossing a bridge when it went down. As the bridge dropped beneath him, Keith jumped out of the truck and climbed to safety. The vehicle was washed away and demolished. The Mechams also lost all their stacks of hay that were in the field, plus their new tractor-rake. Their property was under six feet of water. I guess I don't have to tell you what a flood can do to a plowed field. Their land was covered with all kinds of debris. When Floyd was asked what he'd do about losing so much, he just replied, "Oh, we'll just start over. It won't take long."

Take care, Carolyn

It took several weeks for most people to return to normal living. Treks to the Bella Coola townsite were for necessary supplies only. It took several hours just to get there because of the many ferry crossings.

In time, temporary one-way bridges replaced ferries and eventually those gave way to larger two-lane bridges. Everyone breathed a heavy sigh of relief when the flood of '65 was over. I, for one, would never see the Bella Coola River in the same light as before. I now knew the river was like a sleeping giant, one that could be awakened, anytime the right conditions prevailed. I knew I never wanted to see the giant again.

Sometime in early November, we received word that my sister Phyllis, Johnny's mother, would be joining us in Bella Coola. I responded to one of her letters:

Dear Phyllis,
So glad you're finally coming north. Don't worry that we don't have a library in the Valley. I have found that most people have their own books and will often share them. I've also heard that there is a way to order books from a place in Victoria. They ship books via Northland Prince and it docks at the wharf. So, don't worry about becoming "bushed".

I'm sending some money in hopes that you can pick up some make-up for me. I can't believe Sandy and I are the only women who wear make-up. They don't even sell it at the local Co-op.

See you soon, Carolyn

I knew that before long, my brother Bob, his wife Shirley, and their four children would also be making the long journey north. Dave and I felt pressured to find a place to live so we could help other family members who would soon be arriving. With this in mind, the Andy Widsten house was becoming more and more attractive all the time.

Dave reluctantly agreed to talk to Andy and go over our proposed agreement. He also agreed to talk to Elmer Sollid.

Andy re-affirmed the details and offered to co-sign for Dave at the local credit union so the loan could pay Andy for the house and land.

Dave, still dragging his feet, went on to discuss the moving of the gigantic house with Elmer. He couldn't have met up with a more positive, happy-go-lucky kind of a guy. After much speculation the two reached a decision. Elmer thought we had a 50/50 chance of landing the house on our property with the roof still intact. That was good enough for Dave. He decided it was worth a try.

Dave and I examined the five acres that we had agreed to buy from Andy. The land bordered a high mountain on the south side where a beautiful waterfall trickled downward from a 6000-foot rock face. To the east, a large grassy meadow provided a lovely view. It didn't take us long to determine where the house would sit.

The five acres also had a good stand of timber on it. Dave determined he could do a select logging operation, only removing what was needed, and the sale of the timber would provide funds to pay Elmer's wages. The plan sounded pretty simple, but of course it wasn't.

In the meantime, Andy agreed to let us live at the old homestead until we could make all the necessary arrangements to move the house.

Excited about the new venture, we packed our belongings and moved into the largest house we'd ever lived in.   Later, Dave and Elmer began formulating and fine-tuning their plans.

They agreed they'd need some more help, so Elmer recruited Albert White who was well known for his ability to work through difficult projects. His expertise and knowledge would offer needed support for the success of their mission.

One thing in their favor was the new floor joists installed by Andy just a few years earlier. They would offer much needed strength to the base of the house when it was lifted off its old foundation.

First, a trench had to be dug around the base of the house. To accomplish this, the front and back porches had to be dismantled and torn down.   They would be replaced when the house was settled on its new resting site, and when we could afford it.

Next, the tedious job of jacking the house up commenced. It just so happened that Elmer had a shed full of house jacks. He felt the 10-, 20-, and 50-ton monster jacks would provide the necessary lifting power that was required. Without them, the job would've been impossible.

Each jack was placed at necessary increments, then jacked up a few inches, providing room for blocks to be placed underneath the house. This process was a lengthy one and took several weeks to complete.

It was difficult to enter or exit the house, so it was necessary to lay a long plank over the moat-like trench.   The incline of the plank became steeper each day as the house moved upward.

At the new site, Sy Nystrom moved his D-6 Cat onto the property to clear a house pad. The men formed up and poured a septic tank using a hand mixer. Then Albert fell two large spruce trees. Sy yarded them with his Cat across the road and over the Widsten meadow, the length of two football fields. Each tree was four feet in diameter and seventy feet long. They were placed parallel, one to the other, beneath the house. The house was then lowered onto the timbers and took on a sleigh-like appearance when the house and skid-runners became one.

Next, two sturdy hemlock trees were felled, then winched over the road and down the meadow to the project. These were placed perpendicular to the two spruce skids. They were strapped down with logging cables and acted as braces. A bridle fashioned out of logging cable was formed, so the D-6 Cat could attach and pull the giant sleigh.

Elmer, Albert and Dave were content with the project on the Snootli Stretch. Now, they would have to wait for a cold spell to set in. The plan was to flood the large meadow with irrigation water from a nearby ditch, which in turn would freeze. The field would then become a gigantic ice skating rink helping to slide our sleigh-like house.

I'm sure the three men understood exactly what they were doing as they went about their business, but the venture on the Snootli Stretch was getting a lot of attention from Valley skeptics who now began to scoff at the whole operation.

As one taunting local put it: "You see, the way it works is, when you move, you pack your things and move. You don't pack your house and move. Ha, ha, ha."

It had been necessary to discuss work plans over the telephone during the evening hours. Dave had no idea that curious party-line members couldn't resist listening in on the details of the project.

The phone company had seven lines. One was reserved solely for the Royal Canadian Mounted Police. Another one was for the Bella Coola Hospital. Each of the remaining lines were divided up for residential use. That meant telephone lines had at least twenty four party-line members, and it was possible to have several curious, silent listeners secretly taking part while people talked. The encroachment on private information was called "rubber-necking".

The old-fashioned system had plagued me from the start, and the archaic method of calling a home on our party-line was just too ridiculous to believe. It required several different ring sequences of long or short to identify who the intended receiver was. For example: One of my dreaded rings was four long and four short. I would pick up the phone, listen to see if the line was free, (most often it wasn't) then I would place my hand on the ringer, turn it ringgggg, ringgggg, ringgggg, ringgggg then ring, ring, ring, ring. This required concentrated effort just to get the right intervals of long and short sounds. Also, I had to hurry so the next person waiting to use the line couldn't ring in ahead of me.

If I was calling someone on a different line other than my own, I simply waited for the operator to say "Operator" and I responded "4-Y," then she would ring it for me, if that line wasn't busy. Oftentimes she would startle me by saying, "No use ringing that number, I saw them go down the road a few minutes ago."

If a long-distance call had to be placed, we traveled to the telephone office in Hagensborg. It took several minutes to complete a call. The local operator had to crank an old-time ringer to connect with a Williams Lake operator who in turn placed the call. Then the local operator collected the charges right after we were through talking.

The telephone office was open from 8:00 a.m. to 10:00 p.m. daily, and in-between those hours, the only person we could call was someone on our own line. With the many rings being cranked out in an endless array of coded sounds all day, plus a few on-line callers late at night, our phone was a very busy instrument.

Dave and I had not yet developed the art of "rubber-necking," but it became very obvious to us that other people had. There were those who knew as much about the Snootli Stretch venture as the ones discussing it.

We also learned there were several jokes going around about the giant sleigh-house that was to be skidded over an ice field. Some had even placed bets on whether the 65-year-old house would still be standing by the time it finished its infamous ride. It was Elmer who brought this to our attention one morning. Dave and I must have looked a little forlorn about the news.

"Oh well," Elmer said. "I still think you'll be the winners when everything is done. You still have a 50/50 chance of pulling it off, eh?"

Dave and I tried to keep a low profile during the next few weeks as we took care of miscellaneous things around the place, and waited for our cold spell to set in. Everything would remain in the house, but we thought it a good idea to cover the furniture, and secure all the cupboards and doors. Anything breakable was placed in a box.

It was bad enough to face the fact we'd become the object of much ridicule, but to make matters worse, Ted Brooks, caretaker of the Widsten homestead, refused to speak to us or even acknowledge we existed. I tried every way to befriend him, but it became very plain to me he had absolutely no use for the crazy young Americans who'd moved onto the Widsten homestead. I later mentioned this problem to the butcher at the Hagensborg store, George Robson, who was one of the few people who really knew Ted. I felt badly and didn't understand why Ted hated us so.

"You've destroyed his world. All he cares about is that old homestead, eh? It will never be the same for him."

I was a little surprised at George's comment but pondering it in my mind, I knew he was right. We had invaded a very private sanctuary and were considered trespassers.

"He also dislikes women. He had a bad experience once and chooses to live his life as a hermit, eh?"

When I returned home that day I felt like the world had been placed on my shoulders. I didn't intentionally want to hurt anyone. It was bad enough having all the interest surrounding our house-moving project, and now this.

I sat staring out the kitchen window. Then I saw Ted pull into the driveway in his old English-model pickup truck. He parked the vehicle in the shed that he'd instructed us was off limits.

I walked to the door and turned the knob. "Ted," I yelled.

I balanced myself as my rotund, nine-months pregnant body waddled across the plank stretched across the trench. I moved slowly while walking down the ramp and looked up only once to see if he would wait for me. Ted stood there watching, perhaps to witness my demise, should I fall into the trench. Finally, I caught up to him and stood in front of him looking deep into his eyes.

"Ted, I'm sorry that we've disrupted your home. I didn't realize how much this old place means to you. If it's any consolation, I just want you to know that I love this old house and I plan to take very good care of it."

A strange look came over Ted's face, but he didn't say a word. He quickly turned around and walked toward the meadow and path that led to his cabin. I had tried to make him understand. That was all I could do. I walked back to the house and once again did my balancing act to regain entry into the house.

Several days later, as I walked from the living room into the kitchen, I was startled to find Ted standing in the house next to the kitchen door. He hadn't even knocked. I held my breath for a moment and wasn't sure why he'd entered the house.

"I brought you some apples," Ted said in a heavy Australian accent.

I looked down at the floor where I saw a box of red apples.

"From the root cellar," he explained, looking down at the box.

I smiled at the sight of the beautiful apples. "Thanks Ted."

He turned and walked out the door.

Suddenly, I felt so much better. This one small exchange meant a great deal to me. I knew that Ted had forgiven us.

The long-awaited cold spell set in. Dave released the water from the irrigation ditch and flooded the field. Our ice rink began to form as ice developed. Two days later, Sy Nystrom moved his D-6 Cat back to the old homestead.

Looking out the window that cold wintry morning, I saw a long line of trucks and cars already lined up to watch the parade. I could feel butterflies forming in my stomach as I started biting on a fingernail. Suddenly, I wanted Dave to take me to the Crown Zellerbach house. I knew I didn't have enough fingernails, on two hands, to get me through this nerve-racking day.

"Well, we'll either have a very big house on five acres at the end of this day, or we'll have the biggest darn bonfire anyone ever saw," Dave told me as we drove in the driveway at the Crown Zellerbach house.

"I hope we have the big house on five acres, but just in case, I'm going over to the Hagensborg store and get some weenies and marshmallows. Good luck," I said, and Dave drove away.

Returning to the project, Dave began the last minute preparations. An employee from B.C. Hydro had to be stationed with a long pole to lift the power lines over the house as it traversed from the ice rink onto the asphalt road. He would accomplish this by sitting on the roof of the moving house.

Mack Gurr was concerned about Cat tracks on the asphalt so a series of rubber tires were placed on the road for the Cat to crawl over. The skids carrying the weight of the house weren't expected to cause any damage.

Everything was finally ready. People stood alongside the road watching in anticipation. Sy tightened the slack on the cable-bridle. He placed the Cat in gear and tried to loosen the runner-skids from the frozen ground. It took several attempts before the house-sleigh started inching its way across the iced-over meadow and toward its future resting site.

Once the house started moving, it continued its trek across the frozen ground. Dave walked slowly next to the massive dwelling as it steadily progressed over the ice. He focused on any new sound that might warn of a sudden change. So far, everything was just fine. Dave began to feel the excitement of the adventure taking place before his eyes.

Suddenly, Sy adjusted the Cat's direction 90 degrees, but the house continued its westerly motion with no regard for its leader. The Cat continued its corrected path and eventually the cable arc tightened. Ever so gradually, it tugged at the house until it started moving in the right direction. The delayed action of the house righting itself was done with precision accuracy. Sy had known just the right maneuver, at just the right time.

Sy eased the Cat up to the road and stopped. The house continued to slide slowly across the ice, but came to a standstill when it approached the steep incline just before the road.

The B.C. Hydro employee climbed to the roof and sat on his perch with pole in hand. Traffic was halted in both directions on the road. It didn't matter because no one wanted to go anywhere. A crucial part of the move was coming up. Would the structure's frame survive the upward climb to the surface of the road?

The Cat engine was started once more and Sy crawled across the tires. Inch by inch, the house started up the embankment. Everyone listened for structural groaning. None could be heard. The house reached the pavement and its skid-runners slid onto the asphalt surface. The power lines were lifted. All was going just as planned, then suddenly, the chimney collapsed and came crashing down. The deafening sound of hundreds of bricks falling inside the house made a dreadful sound. Bricks falling on the outside hit the roof with such a force, Dave was sure all would be lost.

Quickly, Elmer reassured everyone he expected the chimney to fall. Everything was still OK.

The house continued to move across the road. Sy tightened the cable slack and pulled onto the meadow. When the skids came to a halt, the bridle was removed then re-connected at the opposite end. The Cat and sleigh-house started moving once more. Slowly, the Cat eased its heavy burden onto a new resting place.

A loud cheer went up from all those who won the bet. They were Elmer, Albert and Dave.

6

The Galvanized #3 Tub

When I approached the Snootli Stretch the next day, I could see that the old homestead appeared void and lacked identity, as if a vital part had been plucked out. On the other side of the road, nestled back in the trees, I could see the old house in its new scenic backdrop. It looked strange to me, as if its old character had been miraculously transformed.

The house-moving project now complete, our attention focused on all the necessary repairs. Our first priority was heating the house due to the collapse of the old chimney. Even if it had survived, we couldn't risk undetected fractures in the framework. Before long, we had a new and safe stainless steel chimney installed.

Crumbling bricks and mortar from the old chimney left masonry residue and soot all over everything in the house. It created a clean-up project of astronomical proportions, one that took several weeks.

Next, we considered the issue of water and power. Unable to dig a well in frozen ground, we were facing the chore of hauling household water from the Snootli Creek in five gallon containers. This also meant doing laundry the old fashioned way, with a scrub-board, using as little water as possible. Used wash-water would then be utilized to flush the toilet so we could maintain our indoor facility. Telephone and electrical lines were temporarily out of the question due to the cost of establishing new lines from the main road.

Still, we continued to bask in the glow of our great house-moving accomplishment and were excited about owning our first home. We were determined to enjoy it, no matter what. We used kerosene lamps for lighting, and learned how to stoke a wood fire to keep it built-up and burning to provide necessary heat. We packed water from streams and occasionally from a neighbor's house. We learned that we could survive without a phone. But, I can honestly say, I never did get used to the scrub-board routine and every laundry day was truly a chore. The paradox was, even though we lived within reach of amenities that would enhance our lifestyle, we didn't have the means to acquire them.

We seemed to blend right in, though, for many of the old-time residents lived under similar circumstances. Traditionally, when a young couple married, they established a home by whatever means they could, then moved in. This was usually a shell of a house, maybe even a garage, with no water, power or telephone. The rest of their married life was spent adding on or improving their home as funds became available. Simple living conditions were considered normal. Those fortunate enough to have running water usually had an old wringer-style washer, and no one had a clothes dryer. Clothes were always dried either on a hanging rack inside, or on a clothes line outside. It was considered wasteful to dry them any other way.

Credit purchases were unheard of because no one had credit cards; however, groceries could be charged at the local Co-op and the Hagensborg Store, if necessary. Also, Mecham's Sales and Service, the local fuel distributor, allowed charges. "Charging" for the necessities of life had long been established due to "shut down" of logging operations, and the two terms seemed to go hand-in-hand. There was no unemployment insurance fund in British Columbia--it had long been exhausted. Families survived the best way they could until logging operations started once again. Then they had to work the rest of the year just to catch up on last year's accrued charges.

We were very fortunate that first winter because Dave landed a part-time job at Mecham's Sales and Service pumping gas and delivering fuel oil. He worked for Aunt Isabell's two brothers, Jim and Albert, whom he liked very much. He also enjoyed working with Frank Cook, the mechanic. The wages weren't too terrific. Most of the time they were exchanged for a free tank of gasoline or stove oil, but somehow we managed to get by.

Chilling temperatures brought plenty of snow and as it piled up outside, we hunkered in like hibernating bears. The freezing wind that occasionally hit the valley was called the East Wind, but we learned that it was really the north wind, or arctic wind. Funneling through the east/west valley, it picked up momentum with each mile, and became a bitter-cold blast that left people house-bound for days at a time.

We closed off the upstairs part of the house because it became impossible to heat both levels. The only way I could keep warm downstairs was to wear leotards on my legs with long johns over them. Then I piled on warm clothing of long pants and flannel shirts. Now I understood why the dining room had been converted into a downstairs bedroom. One week of east wind and twenty degrees below zero would convince anyone to stay close to their best friend, the warm stove.

The oil stove in the kitchen kept the back part of the house warm, but it was absolutely mandatory that the wood stove in the front part of the house stay ablaze, just to keep the chill off the other rooms. Every time Dave left the house, he reminded me to keep adding logs to the fire. It seemed a simple thing to do, but I wasn't used to working so hard at maintaining warmth in a house. I also wasn't used to building a new fire each time the old one burned out.

There were times when it seemed difficult to adapt to the old lifestyle that we'd chosen. Each day seemed to bring new challenges.

On one occasion, I forgot to check the fire. When I finally remembered, it was too late. I opened the cast iron door on the stove and prayed for a smoldering ember, but I couldn't be so lucky. I blew on unresponsive ashes that showed no life. I opened the draft by turning the round metal plate. Nothing. I turned the damper vertically at the flue. Still nothing.

"OK," I told myself, "It can't be that difficult to build a fire. I've seen Dave do it a hundred times."

I crumpled up paper and stacked it on the soft ashes. Next, I chopped small slivers of wood with a hand ax and placed them on the paper. I staggered several small pieces of wood forming a pile of artistic design. Things were looking good and my confidence grew as I looked in on my creation. Now, for the kerosene bottle. I gently poured fuel over each piece of wood. I wasn't sure how much to pour out so I poured plenty. Looking in on the stack, I decided to place two large pieces of wood on top to insure quick ignition. I looked at the damper. "Open or shut?" I asked myself. I couldn't remember what Dave did at this point. I looked at the draft with its circular plate. "Open or shut?" A quick decision was made, "Shut," and I closed both tightly. I was a little concerned about having enough kerosene on the wood so I added some more. I then closed the air-tight door and latched it securely. Now all I needed was a match.

It took several minutes to find a new package of wooden matches while rummaging through the kitchen cupboards. Tearing the wrapper off, I then slid the cover open, exposing the sticks with red and white colored tips. Walking back to the living room, I decided there really wasn't anything to building a fire.

On the top of the stove, I found a small hole about the size of a pea. I wasn't sure what its purpose was but it looked like a good place to drop a match. I struck the match against the sandpaper surface on the side of the box, leaned over, and dropped the match into the tiny hole.

What happened next was a complete surprise. The combustion that was created when the flame met built-up fumes and oiled-down kindling was truly amazing. The power of the explosion blasted the top circular plate off the stove. At the same time, the flue vent exploded open spraying soot from the stove-pipe all over everything in a six-foot radius.

I felt like I'd witnessed a volcanic eruption. When I looked in the mirror hanging on the wall across the room, I could see my face and hair were blackened by soot, and when I moved, fine particles of debris fell from my head. My glaring white eyeballs appeared three times normal size while staring in disbelief.

I looked at the cast iron plate on the floor ten feet away and was thankful it hadn't hit me. I slowly bent over to peer down into the metal cavity. There wasn't even a flicker of a flame. I couldn't believe it.

It took all day to clean up the room and to make matters worse, I had to listen to Dave grumble and groan through gritted teeth when he had to build a fire to warm up the cold house. I felt really bad and decided no matter what, I would keep Dave's morning fire burning. That was the least I could do.

It became a quest. I worked on this simple task by using all kinds of reminders: string on the finger, notes on the ice-box and wood stacked in conspicuous places. It took some effort but I soon learned I could keep the fire going.

Dave let his hair grow long for extra warmth and he also grew whiskers on his face. I learned to keep a chamber pot under the bed for nighttime use. During those long winter months, I found myself constantly looking out the window for any sign of change. Spring was a long time coming.

While cleaning upstairs one day, I noticed that two of the bedrooms appeared to have a concealed dead space in-between, because their walls didn't join. Standing in the hallway, I moved my hands over the surface of the wall. I could feel two cracks running vertically up the wall as if someone had boarded up a room. I quickly loosened the boards by pulling out some loose nails holding them in place.

When I finally removed the barrier, I could see an attic room cluttered with old stored items. By then, my curiosity had gotten the best of me, so I lit a kerosene lamp and peered into the newly discovered room. Shocked by what I saw, I stood motionless. There in the corner of the room was a hand-crafted antique pump organ, all covered in dust. I beamed with delight and could hardly wait for Dave to return home so I could share the news with him.

Evenings took on a whole new significance. Dave pumped and played the organ as I sat next to the kerosene lamp and crocheted. We had no modern-day newspaper, television or radio to inform or entertain us, and we felt as though we'd traveled back in time, to a place where the simple, old-fashioned lifestyle was still cherished.

How well I remember the night when I went into labor with our first child. The wind was blowing and snow was falling when, around midnight, Dave ran outside to start the truck and discovered a flat tire, with no spare. Running for the Dorsey's house a mile away, Dave begged to borrow their car. Mike Dorsey was hesitant to loan his only vehicle because his wife Gayle was also due to deliver, and she had already made one trip to the hospital with false labor pains. But, he finally gave in, making Dave promise to come right back after dropping me off at the hospital in Bella Coola.

Giant snow flakes had already covered Dave's footprints on the roadway as he cautiously drove back to the house. The eight mile trip to Bella Coola was a little scary with slick roads, me in labor and a very nervous first-time father at the wheel of a strange vehicle. Eventually, we made it safely to the hospital, then Dave turned around and drove the slick road once more, returning to the Dorsey's as promised. It was early the next morning when he finally got the flat tire fixed and returned to the hospital for the second time.

The Bella Coola Hospital was an old two-story building providing a public clinic and pharmacy in the downstairs area. The upstairs was the actual hospital. It was small but adequate. I learned that people living in more remote areas than Bella Coola, up to 300 miles away, often traveled by way of float plane just to receive medical services. I had to laugh when I pictured pregnant women flying in for a delivery.

By late afternoon, my sense of humor had faded. Gerti, the nurse, held my left hand while Dave held my right. Doctor Crosby finally arrived and immediately he started discussing how great Dave's nose looked. It had healed up nicely with very little scarring. Doctor Crosby gave me a quick check and decided "we" were getting close. He and Dave then proceeded to discuss God's greatest gift.

"How big was that Spring Salmon you caught last year up by Stuie?" Dave asked the doctor. "I heard it was a big one."

"It was a forty pounder and a feisty bugger. One of the largest Springs ever caught in the Valley, eh? It gave me the thrill of my life, catching it on 30 pound test line." Doctor Crosby seemed to beam while telling the details of his great catch.

Then he asked Dave, "Have you been out beating the river?"

"Yeah," Dave said, "I went out with Harold and Arnie Hansen the other day. They finally took me to their secret fishing hole, and I caught a gorgeous seventeen-pound steelhead. Not anywhere as big as your Spring but it sure fought back and was awfully good eating."

Doctor Crosby responded, "I really enjoy steelhead. They put up a good fight."

The two men paused for a moment while I suffered through a labor pain. Then Dave started in again.

"Ernie Sollid and I made a trip out the inlet to Green River, out by Masachie Nose a while back. We caught and released some great steelhead, all fifteen to twenty-five pounders."

"I've been wanting to make a trip out there but I've heard the bear population is terrible," Doctor Crosby replied.

"You're right, it's hard to fish and watch for bears at the same time," Dave agreed.

There was a pause for a labor pain.

Dave continued, "The funniest thing happened to me over at Walker Island. I pulled in there, got out of the truck, and quickly made three casts into the river. I caught three steelhead, one with each cast. Each fish weighed about seventeen pounds."

A long pause for a labor pain.

"When I loaded up the truck to leave, I noticed that three tourists were standing to one side watching. As I drove off, I looked in my rear-view mirror and all I could see were three mouths hanging open. I think they wanted to know what I used on the end of that line."

"What did you use on the end of that line?" Doctor Crosby asked staring at Dave.

Well, that did it. I couldn't take any more fish stories or labor pains so I decided to get it over with. The real catch of the day was a little girl named Pam from the German-English human species weighing in at a whopping 9 pounds 5 ounces. And yes, she gave me quite a fight.

Exhausted from fishing stories, labor pains, and the delivery, I was content to rest in bed while Dave and Doctor Crosby continued to discuss great catches.

"Have you heard about the twenty-pound Spring Salmon my wife Anne caught?" the Doctor asked. "You'll have to hear her story."

Finally, Doctor Crosby invited Dave to dinner at his home. The two avid fisherman must have talked into the wee hours of the morning because Dave ended up spending the night. Anne, also a fishing enthusiast, told her story about going into labor while landing a twenty-pound salmon. She stayed with the fish, even when her water broke. Her husband aided her in landing the beauty, then quickly made a mad dash for the hospital some twenty-five miles away.

Meanwhile, I laid back in my hospital bed and realized that every muscle in my body felt wrenched. After identifying the source of my pain, I knew that it wasn't "just" from giving birth. I couldn't help but grimace when I remembered, in detail, the events of the previous day when I decided to take a bath.

Normally, I bathed in the bathroom, but the room was too cold. I decided the living room was a much warmer place to take a bath. Standing next to the wood stove, I patiently responded each time the kettle whistled with hot bubbly water. Gradually, I filled a galvanized number 3 tub sitting next to the stove. I remembered bathing in a number 3 tub when I was a child. Being several years older, nine months pregnant and thirty pounds heavier than normal, I should've reconsidered bathing in the small tub.

Upon seating myself down into the water, I suddenly realized there was no room for my legs and arms. This was going to be a quick bath. After scrubbing the best I could, I tried to lean forward and lift myself up to climb out of the tub. I couldn't move. I tried to get lift-off from the floor by pushing with both hands. Still, my overweight torso wouldn't budge. I resembled a turtle, turned on its shell, helplessly trying to free itself. After several minutes, I knew there was no way out of the tub. I was stuck.

The fire in the stove was dying down. "Oh no, the fire will go out," I blurted out loud.

There was a stack of wood next to the stove. With a lot of effort on my part, I picked up a log between my two feet and lifted it toward the front opening of the stove. All I needed now was something to open the door. Fortunately, a metal poker lay on the floor within reaching distance. I stretched as far as my bulging, rotund belly would allow and managed to open the metal door. Then I pushed the wood into the opening. I was sure the closing door would inch the log forward into the fire. I was thankful I could keep the fire going even though I was confined. The water in the tub was turning cold.

I had never felt so helpless in all my life. I stared down at my protruding bulk of a belly and my arms and legs hanging helplessly over the top edge of the tub. I started counting stretch marks on my tummy and was truly amazed at how many there were. In my disgust, I reached over and picked up a terry towel then placed it over my body. I was surprised at how much warmer I felt.

I had come to the conclusion my only choice was to wait for Dave to come home. He'd have to help me out of the tub. It would be about an hour and I prayed I wouldn't go into labor in the meantime. I was becoming very sore and stiff in my uncomfortable position. As if things weren't bad enough, I suddenly remembered that Dave mentioned he might bring home a friend. I felt sick just thinking about this so I tried once more to lift myself up. It was no use.

It was time for another log. I managed this task with a little effort and a big sliver in my toe. But at least the fire was still burning.

It seemed like an eternity had passed when I finally heard Dave at the kitchen door.

"Are you alone?" I yelled from the living room.

Dave strolled cautiously toward me. "What are you doing?" he asked, surprised at the sight before him.

"I'm taking a bath, what do you think? I hope you're alone."

"Yeah, I'm alone," Dave said, staring at me.

"Then help me out of this galvanized trap and cold water."

Tears were beginning to well-up and I couldn't hold them back any longer. Dave helped me out of the tub by lifting and pulling. It took some effort on his part but finally I was freed.

It was such a relief to be out of the tub, but it took several minutes before my stiff, pregnant body would walk upright. Every muscle in my body felt wrenched. Fortunately, Dave went outside for awhile so I could regain my composure.

Later that night, as we lay in bed, Dave thanked me for keeping the fire going that day. I thanked him for not bringing a friend home. He patted my stomach and thanked the baby for not

being born that day. We both chuckled for a bit
before falling off into a deep sleep.

7

DAVE KISSES THE BEAR

Canadian officials marveled as Bella Coola-bound landed immigrants arrived at their border. The possibility of a gold strike must have entered their minds.

My sister Phyllis Thomas immigrated north just before Christmas of 1965 and experienced a unique problem at the border. As a single parent, with no visible means of support, immigration officials required a sponsorship by a Canadian citizen. Mack Gurr became that sponsor when he committed to support Phyllis and Johnny if she couldn't find work. Accustomed to supporting herself, Phyllis' main concern was finding a job. She was fortunate to land a position right away working as a telephone operator for the Bella Coola Telephone Company. She and Johnny rented the upstairs portion of the Crown Zellerbach house, and before long, Phyllis adapted to the new lifestyle.

Brother Bob and his wife Shirley, their four children Mike, Scott, Steven, and Terry Lynn, arrived in the Valley the following summer. They were pleased to find the old Olsen house for rent in Hagensborg. The Olsens had built a newer home. Soon Bob was working as a mechanic for Norm Saugstad at the Hagensborg Garage.

Later that summer, my mother and father, Bud and Grace Shelton, and my nine-year-old sister Cindy, moved to the Valley. My parents landed a job managing Sy Nystrom's new cafe in the upper Valley and lived on Sy's property in a little cabin only a short distance from the Bella Coola River.

The family migration north to Bella Coola was now complete. Gradually, everyone settled in and adjusted to the new lifestyle.

Gary and Sandy bought a large parcel of land with 160 acres and river frontage. The property was at the base of Mount Nusatsum. Gary soon built a small cabin to live in until a larger house could be built.

My parents bought six acres across the road from Gary's place. They cleared the land, put in a large vegetable garden, and made plans to build a house the following year.

Bob obtained permission to clean up all the bridge timbers that washed ashore during the flood. He determined he could construct a small cabin out of the salvage project because of the large quantity of timbers. His cabin was built on my parent's land in a large stand of cedar. It was a very sturdy structure and we all referred to it as the "bridge house". Bob felt the timbers had proven worthy; after all, they had survived a flood.

Meanwhile, Dave and I adjusted to our changing lifestyle with a new baby daughter. We enjoyed our new role as parents very much, and we both took turns seeing to her needs.

We were very surprised when we received the bill for the baby's delivery and my seven-day stay in the hospital. The total bill was only $7, one dollar for each day of care. The new-mother pampering period was truly a necessity because most women had so few luxuries at home.

Later, when Dave went to pay the bill, Doctor Crosby informed him that if the fee was too much, a smaller bill could be negotiated. Dave thanked the good doctor and insisted it was more than fair. Besides, when Dave spent the night at the Crosby's, he got the doctor to divulge his secret fishing hole. Dave thought that information alone was well worth every penny of the seven dollars.

Gayle Dorsey had arrived at the hospital just a few hours after me and gave birth to a little boy named Sam. It was fun having a roommate and we got quite a kick out of watching Pam and Sam in the nursery; he in his blue blanket and she in her pink one. Gayle and I were almost related. Her mother, Leora, was my Aunt Isabell's sister.

Dave continued to upgrade our place the best way he could as funds became available. All the sub-flooring in the downstairs area was replaced. Clearing trees from around the house, Dave then utilized them for necessary firewood. He purchased lumber from the local Northcop Sawmill to build a shed, obtaining most of the materials at dirt-cheap prices. The purchased lumber was referred to as culls, but in the States, the same material would've easily passed as quality construction grade.

The shed measured 12 by 24 feet. A good portion was used for storing cordwood for winter fuel. Bob donated his labor to help Dave, and the whole project cost less than $300.

Soon, Albert White fell the selected timber on our property which was later sold. This brought in some money, but due to a decline in the demand for lumber, profits were less than hoped for. Douglas fir had dropped from $50 to $35 per thousand board foot. Consequently, replacing the front and back porches had to be postponed, so the sturdy wooden stairs at each entry would have to make do.

It was the Canadian custom to always enter a house from the back through a mud room or porch where shoes were removed. Our kitchen became the main entryway and shoes stacked up at the door while visitors took on a comfortable-looking pose in stocking feet.

We received many gifts for the new baby, most of which had been hand-knitted or crocheted. Our little Pam was decked out in some of the finest homemade baby clothes ever worn. When Mack and Ruth stopped by to see the new baby, I thought I saw a special gleam in Ruth's eye. I could tell right away she loved new babies. I wasn't too surprised when nine months later she gave birth to their sixth child named Kenny.

I washed diapers by hand every day using the scrub board. There was no such thing as disposable diapers and even if there had been, they would've cost far too much.

We soon discovered our newly purchased land was inhabited by many small creatures such as squirrels and rabbits. Many species of birds liked to drop by looking for food, and we especially enjoyed watching the majestic Trumpeter Swans as they assembled on the front meadow. We also got a kick out of watching the river otters as they romped their way through the trees.

One afternoon, as I walked through the kitchen, I saw an animal run beneath the table. Investigating further, I discovered a small ermine. She was so petite and delicate with her snow-white fur and black-tipped tail. It didn't take long to get used to her and soon she became a household pet. We found she could enter and exit the house whenever she pleased through a small hole in the floor under the kitchen sink. I made sure she had plenty of nibblies to munch on and I decided to call her Prissy. I was a little surprised one day when a professional photographer, visiting the Valley, knocked on our door and asked if he could take pictures of our pet ermine. I was happy to oblige but Prissy proved far too shy to be photographed by a stranger.

When spring finally rolled around, Prissy took on a whole new look when her fur changed color from white to brown, but the black tip on her tail remained the same. One day while washing dishes, I heard a strange racket coming from under the sink. When I opened the cupboard door, I couldn't believe my eyes. A large ball of brown fur wreathed and twisted as two weasels mated. When they finally separated, the male ran out into the kitchen and I got a good look at Prissy's new boyfriend. I could see that unlike the female of the species, he took on a fierce appearance with thick, mane-like fur around the neck. He was at least three times bigger than Prissy and there wasn't anything cute or friendly about him. At once I gave him the nickname Little Devil.

I ran toward Little Devil and on my way grabbed a small cardboard box in hopes of catching him. He ran from me, darting around corners with unexpected lightning speed. He dashed toward the bedroom where four-month-old Pam lay sleeping on my bed. Little Devil leaped for the dresser, hit into the wall, then turned as if he was going to attack me. Suddenly, he jumped toward the bed, leaping high in the air like a flying squirrel. When he descended, he was about to land on my sleeping baby. A mother's protective instinct must have kicked in because I leaped with lightning speed at the same time as Little Devil, and caught the little bugger in mid-air. I fell to the floor so I wouldn't land on Pam. At the same time, Little Devil bit me.

The pain caused by razor-sharp teeth was bad enough, but there was one more indignity to suffer when I learned a very important lesson about the animal. Skunks aren't the only creatures with glands capable of spraying a horrible stench. All of the weasel family are equipped and loaded, and when they get excited, watch out! I gagged and coughed at the terrible odor inflicted just inches from my face. Somehow, I managed to hold onto the animal and put him in the box. I put the lid down and quickly taped it shut.

Later that night, Dave sealed off the exposed area under the sink and we returned Little Devil to the great outdoors where he belonged. I knew Prissy could no longer enter the house. I hated to give her up, but I just couldn't tolerate her boyfriend. Little Devil had left an imprint on my mind as well as my hand.

I thought about the two ermines quite often. Especially when the temperature warmed up in the house. That's when a strong wild odor seemed to exude from the walls of the bedroom.

As time went by, we discovered another resident living on our property--a medium-sized black bear.

On numerous occasions friends had reported seeing a bear in our driveway during daylight hours. One night when we investigated a noise outside, we saw a black bear rummaging through our garbage. After that, we took extra precautions to insure the resident bear didn't read our garbage as a menu and invitation to dinner.

Keeping the wood box full, even in the spring, required a lot of hard work for Dave. The cutting, splitting and stacking of wood took up a lot of his time.

Our woodshed was thirty feet away from the house. Going out in the dark to get wood was risky business because it was easy to trip on the slightest twig, root, or rock along the way. Consequently, Dave tried to bring the wood in during daylight hours. But if he got home late, then he had to stumble out through the dark to find the woodshed.

One evening, Dave prepared to go for wood after dark. I was busy in the kitchen so I didn't watch his departure out the door. Suddenly, I heard the door slam shut. When I turned to inspect the loud bang, I saw Dave with his face as white as a ghost. He was leaning against the closed door as if barricading it from an intruder.

"What happened?" I asked.

"Bear...it was a bear. It was looking in the window on the door...standing on the stairs looking in at us. I stepped into him...my face touched his face...my mouth...his nose."

Dave started rubbing his mouth then ran to the kitchen sink to spit.

"Do you think he's gone?" I asked, looking at the window in the door.

Dave was leaning over the sink and didn't hear me.

"Boy, did he stink...it was awful," he said, wiping his mouth.

Puzzled, I started to imagine what might have happened. Dave must have opened the door suddenly and stepped out. He couldn't see the bear standing on its back feet curiously sniffing at the aroma of cooking fish. I pictured the bear standing with its arms stretched frame-to-frame. Dave would have walked smack into the bear's embrace, colliding with a kiss, then both had instantly jumped for safety. Dave had leaped for the house and the poor bear had leaped for the woods. The bear was probably still running through the woods trying to escape from the human encounter. I looked at Dave who was still spitting. I couldn't help but wonder if somewhere out in the woods, standing by a stream, a very shocked bear was spitting and growling at the thought of kissing a human. It was more than I could take and I burst out laughing.

That was the last time Dave went for wood in the dark.

The much-too-intimate bear kiss wasn't the beginning of Dave's dislike for bears. It started when he and Gary worked in South Bentinck doing the survey work of the proposed logging road for Crown Zellerbach. It was tough enough to work in the windfall and dense undergrowth while pulling a survey chain, but the constant threat of a bear attack couldn't be ignored. The bears were right in the brush with them and they had nothing to use for protection.

There were times they didn't see any bears all day. But they sure heard them. The sound created by large bears crashing through dense jungle just ahead of them made them both very uneasy. The fact the bears were picking up their scent long before they could see them was the only reason they hadn't come face to face with one.

After eating lunch one day, the men left their lunch sacks by a tree and were going to pick them up on their return trip. When they returned to the site, the bears had shredded everything to bits.

Continuing to work, their greatest fear was coming upon a sow with cubs, or a bear protecting a food stash, so they made plenty of noise.

Dave worked out in front of Gary and he'd already figured out who was going to encounter the bear first, should one decide to stand its ground. With so much going on all around them, Dave felt he needed eyes in the back of his head and a climbing tree in sight at all times. The situation just couldn't get any worse.

That's what he thought. Then it started pouring down rain, and the men found themselves slushing through dense jungle, sopping wet, surveying a road as well as surveying for bears.

Dave carried an ax that was used for cutting wedge-shaped sticks. The sticks were to be driven into the ground with a piece of survey ribbon attached. The upper end of the marker was shaved flat so he could write a number on it. While concentrating on a nearby bear one day, Dave accidentally cut his leg open with the ax. It was a bad wound that later became infected. He continued to work while limping his way through the soggy, bear-infested forest.

When the men finally finished the difficult survey work and returned home, they were glad to see civilization again.

The South Bentinck experience had left Gary shaken too. The vulnerability of the situation seemed to light a fire inside. He had developed a keen interest in the fierce animal posing such a threat to them. Gary had grown up on a big ranch in the Sierra-Nevada Mountains of California. He'd been an avid hunter for years and yearned for the day he'd have a bear hide hanging on the wall of his cabin. He studied everything he could find in books regarding bears, talked to many old-timers, and studied bear sign in the woods. Then, he started to hunt for a grizz.

Bear hunting alone is never a good idea so Gary recruited Johnny and Dave to go with him one Sunday. He needed them for back-up should anything unforeseen happen. Dave was brought up to believe that Sunday was a church-going day, and bad things could happen if you chose to do something else on that day. Somehow, with his fear of bears, bear hunting on that day was like asking for the wrath of God to descend upon him. He was afraid that "wrath" might resemble a ferocious, nine-hundred-pound grizzly bear.

The three hunters walked along the calm water below the confluence on the north side of the Bella Coola River. It was fall and dead salmon lay everywhere. Dave held onto a double barrel, twelve gauge shot gun loaded with double-OO buck. Progressing down the trail, the three men could see many fresh piles of bear droppings. Occasionally, a large bear could be heard as it took off running through the closely grown trees and brush. Although they could hear the large animals, they could never get a good look at one. Dave walked in front, praying he wouldn't see a bear, reminiscing on the South Bentinck chain-pulling days when he feared for his life.

They soon entered an over-grown area where the trail narrowed and made a slight curve obstructing visibility ahead. Dave stopped to look down at fresh bear sign on the trail. Suddenly, he heard a noise. Looking up, he saw a large brown beast coming at him. Startled, he raised his gun and pointed it at the animal.

"Don't shoot," a man yelled from a horse.

Dave lowered his gun quickly. The startled horseback rider was Jack Turner, from Turner Lake, leading a pack horse with supplies.

Dave felt sick to his stomach when he realized what almost happened. Right then, he made a promise to himself that he'd gone on his last bear hunt. He wanted nothing more to do with bears.

But, as fate would have it, Dave couldn't avoid the bear population of the Bella Coola area.

It was late fall. Bob, Gary and Dave decided to go deer hunting up the big hill around East Branch. They'd been in such a hurry to get off on the trip they accidentally left all their cooking gear behind. Most of the their food required cooking before eating, so Shirley, Sandy and I had a good laugh over their mistake. The next day, my parents received an urgent message to send pots and pans with Red, the freighter who drove in from Williams Lake each week.

I'd never met the Hodgson Freightway driver who delivered supplies in a five-ton truck as he crossed the Chilcotin. But his name was synonymous with freight and whenever something needed to be shipped in or shipped out, Red always came to mind. He was as well-known as the Simpson-Sears catalog and twice as reliable. Because I'd never seen him, I could only imagine what someone tough enough to drive the grueling road and hill from hell every week would look like. I had a clear mental picture of a large, unshaven, beast-of-a-man all covered in dirt with a chewed-down cigar stub in his mouth. He would be totally immune to pain. His eyes would take on a dazed, blank stare as he feverishly clutched a vibrating steering wheel. I had no doubt his short sleeves were rolled way up exposing bulging biceps and a tattoo that said "Mom". He'd be totally unaware of the persistent, giant mosquitoes in his dust-filled cab. In my mind Red was a legendary character.

My folks dealt with Red on the pots and pans issue, so I never got to meet the infamous freighter. To this day, my vision of him remains the same.

Struggling while cooking over an open fire the best way they could, the hunters were very happy to see Red on his return trip. They now had pans to cook in, but soon realized they were low on food. A quick decision was made to head for Floyd and Inez Mecham's unoccupied summer cabin, in Precipice, where they knew there was a cache of food.

Searching through the Mecham's root cellar, they found crates of straw-covered apples and eggs, plus shelves of canned moose, venison, fruit, and vegetables. The hungry men dined like kings, thanks to Floyd and Inez' unknowing hospitality.

The next afternoon, Bob and Dave wanted to do some hunting around a meadow while Gary went off to explore a timbered area.

Strolling across the meadow, Bob and Dave soon came to a little stream running east to west, and eventually dumping into the Atnarko River.

Following a well-worn cow path, the men noticed that it split, forming two separate trails encircling a thick stand of trees. Bob took the path to the right, while Dave took the left, and soon they could no longer see one another.

Suddenly, Dave heard Bob yell, "There's a bear."

Standing on the opposite side of the thicket, Dave quickly yelled back, "Where?"

"There's a bear," Bob yelled again.

Dave stood frozen, afraid to move, listening for any sound. All at once, he heard a thrashing sound coming through the trees toward him. A huge bear soon appeared. The upset animal seemed as surprised by the intrusion as the men were, and didn't know which way to run.

"There's the bear," Dave yelled, moving away from it.

The men moved toward each other and could finally see the large bear at the same time. Dave had a lever-action, .284 Savage rifle with a five-shot magazine clip. Because he never carried a round in the chamber, his first reaction was to jack a round, so he did. Bob stood just ahead of Dave and the bear was coming toward them. The old .30-06 Remington rifle that Bob carried had a broken ejector pin. He knew he only had one good shot before digging out the spent shell. In split second timing, Bob pointed his gun at the bear. Behind him, he heard Dave jack another round, while ejecting the first. Again, he heard Dave jack another round, while ejecting the second. In all the excitement, Dave had repeated the action three separate times.

Listening to what was going on behind him, and knowing that he had only one shot, Bob was afraid they'd be out of ammo before a second shot could be fired.

Suddenly, the bear ran on past the two men. It was anxious to depart their company. When it cleared the trees, Bob and Dave could see the animal was a beautiful silver-tipped male grizzly in his prime, weighing about 800 pounds. His massive muscles rippled under thick fur as he moved. Soon, the bear reached the crest of a hill just beyond.

The men instantly ran toward the animal, not to harm it, but to watch as its magnificent form descended a 200-foot cliff, crossed over a stream, then scaled up a high mountain. The bear moved unrestrained over the rugged terrain with the speed and force of a locomotive. In twenty seconds flat, the animal gained the same distance that it would take a normal human being forty-five minutes to travel.

Bob and Dave stood in awe of the spectacle. Breathing somewhat easier and relieved at the outcome, they both knew they'd witnessed first hand one of nature's most beautiful sights: THE SOUTH END OF A NORTH BOUND GRIZZLY BEAR!

Carolyn—1961

Carolyn at the Placerville ranch.

Dave
Three casts—three fish.

Mack and Bob's easy hunt.

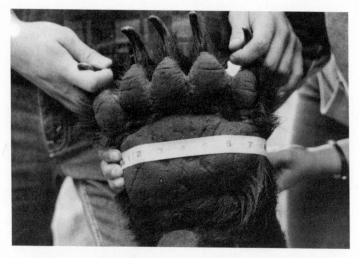

The surrounding coastal rain forest of the Bella Coola area provided the nourishment and genetics to produce immensely large grizzly bears.

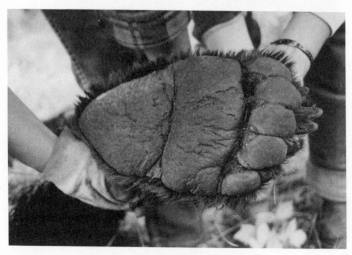

Gary with a problem bear.
Later, Gary trained Government personnel how to survive bear encounters by developing a bear hazard safety training program. In 1994 he became a published author. His book, Bear Encounter Survival Guide, *was a tremendous hit amongst those working in the woods.*

Lige and Isabell Gurr's 50th Wedding Anniversary
Lamont, Betty Jean, Mack, Dean, Buddy, Doug, and Melvin

The Mack Gurr Family
Mike, Barbara, Ruth, Daryl, Mack, Brian
Front row: Sandra and Kenny

The Hill
(KOPAS COLLECTION)

Phyllis Thomas

Barbara Gurr and Johnny Thomas

Angela and Graham Hall

Hard Time Parties:

Ken Phillips and Colleen Nelson

The Bolgers

Men took on a warm healthy glow in their surroundings.
Gary, Bob, Dave and Daryl Gurr

Gary and Sandy cooking fish over open flame.

Placerville—1965

From left: Dave and Carolyn, Gary and Sandy, Bob and Shirley, Bud and Grace, and Johnny.

Children: Steven, Mike, Debbie, Cindy holding Clint, baby Terry Lynn, and Scott

*The beginning of a road—Lige Gurr on Bunchgrass Hill trail—
September 1952.*
(KOPAS COLLECTION)

THE ROAD BUILDERS
Bella Coola road around Anahim Lake.
(KOPAS COLLECTION)

Locals stuck in a boghole.
(KOPAS COLLECTION)

The road from Anahim Lake.
(KOPAS COLLECTION)

Bella Coola Valley
(KOPAS COLLECTION)

BC Packers Cannery
(*Kopas Collection*)

Bella Coola and the Burke Channel Inlet
(KOPAS COLLECTION)

Turner Lake
(KOPAS COLLECTION)

Ulkatcho Natives
(KOPAS COLLECTION)

THE ROAD BUILDERS
Ole Nicoli (foreground) and Melvin Gurr getting ready for another blast.

8

The Rut

At one time, the Anahim Lake area was one of the most densely populated moose habitats on the continent. The rugged terrain with its swamps, pines, willows, and mountains was made-to-order for an animal who lived on willow tops, swamp birch, buck brush, poplar bark and small limbs.

For decades, moose had provided the main source of protein for folks living in the Anahim Lake area and the Bella Coola Valley. For those trying to exist on little or no money, downing a moose every year became a necessity.

Originally, the Chilcotin was inhabited by Caribou instead of moose. As early as 1914, the big flat-horned animals appeared in swamps on the Chilcotin plateau. Then, within a few short years, moose were migrating into the country by the thousands.

Moose became so numerous and so bold that ranchers were forced to pack guns for protection during the October rut. Then in June, after the arrival of the calves, they had to take care to avoid the maternal cow.

Early in September, the bulls leave their feeding grounds to seek out solitary hideouts in inaccessible, harsh terrain. Here, in a land of deadly muskegs, void of all nourishment, the bull moose goes through a metamorphosis.

The self-inflicted starvation diet lasts for two weeks. The bull then reappears with a huge chest and bulging shoulders tapering off into a shrunken belly. The once timid creature is now a red-eyed monster, eager to charge at any object attracting his attention.

The bull is now ready to test out his transformed body on windfalls and trees. He charges and smashes them down with his huge antlers. Then he goes in search of the cows, ready to battle other challengers for the right to mate. During this time, the young bulls are extremely dangerous. Equally as dangerous is the rogue bull, a frustrated old guy who's been defeated in battle by younger and stronger animals. Driven away from the cows, this bad-tempered old warrior slips off to brood, laying in wait for anything to cross his path.

This natural order of events in the untamed world takes place each year. It is called "the rut".

The time had come. It was moose season and city born 23-year-old Dave wanted to bag his first moose. Excited about the hunt, he couldn't wait to place antlers on the wood shed, just above the door. First, he had to find a moose. It would require lots of strenuous effort, hunting in bitter cold and hiking through dark spruce jungles. But, after all, that was just part of the fun.

The concept that moose hunting is fun is a little ridiculous. Moose hunting can be defined by three simple words: REAL HARD WORK. Anyone who has hunted and dressed out a thirteen-hundred pound moose and struggled to get it home will attest to that. And anyone who has come face-to-face with a bull moose in rut has witnessed the violent, ugly side of nature.

Dave drove for a long ways up the Valley hoping to find some sign that would lead him to game. Stopping, he found some hoof prints in the snow leading to a wooded area. There were so many tracks, some deer and some moose, he couldn't tell which were fresh and which were old. Still, it was a well used trail and it was bound to yield something. So Dave parked, prepared his rifle and started hiking on the slippery surface leading into the woods.

Trudging through the snow for a couple of hours, Dave constantly felt the stinging sensation of cold air nipping at his cheeks. After awhile, he stopped and scanned the hillside for any sign of game. Up above, he saw a huge rock slide where there was some kind of movement. Quietly, he sneaked behind a large rock and braced himself so he could peer through his binoculars. Looking at the animals on the hillside, Dave determined it was a herd of deer. Quickly, he changed his stance and lowered his arms. The sudden movement made him lose his footing on the slick surface, so his feet went out from under him. He landed face down in the snow.

The wintry air was already so numbing, he hardly felt the icy snow on his face. Sitting up, he could see his rifle had dug deep into the snow, so he pulled it out. Puckering his lips, he carefully blew off the sites removing any loose snow, then tipped the barrel up to do the same to the bead at the end. Puckering just a little more than he anticipated, when Dave went to blow, his lower lip accidentally made contact with the frozen metal of the gun. Instantly, his lip froze to the gun barrel.

Realizing he had a serious problem, Dave carefully cupped his hands and started breathing hot air over the metal as fast as he could, but with no luck.

Looking for a rock, Dave found a protected cave-like opening where two large rocks came together. At the bottom was an opening large enough to see through to a clearing on the other side. First, he thought he better remove the magazine just to be safe. Then he wrapped his hands around the end of the barrel for insulation, and breathed as heavy as he could trying to defrost it. He continued his huffing, puffing and defrosting for quite sometime.

When Dave stopped his defrosting procedure to breath normally for a moment, he heard a strange sound. Carefully, Dave stood up while holding the gun stuck to his mouth. He looked to see if the deer were coming down from the hill. From this vantage point, he could see they were still in the same place. Then, he heard the strange noise again, only this time, it was louder and closer. Dave couldn't imagine what would make such a loud thumping and thrashing, but whatever it was, it was real mad about something.

Dave lowered himself back down to his protective shelter. It was then he noticed movement on the other side of the rock through the opening. At first, all he could see were four legs. Stooping as far as the gun would allow, he could see the entire body of an animal. But was this the body of an animal or Lucifer in disguise?

The horrible-looking creature was pounding the ground with razor-sharp hoofs while bleating a horrific cry, sending chills down Dave's back. The animal displayed flaring nostrils that puffed out steaming breath clouds, while the hair on its neck stood straight up. Its little rattle-snake eyes stared sharply at something Dave couldn't see. Leaning further to one side, he could see another creature with the same horrible-looking face.

Surely this wasn't the animal he was hunting. Moose were suppose to be similar to deer, only larger.

Dave watched from his protective cave, feeling the ground shake every time the huge giants crashed their antlers together. With nostrils flared and ears laid back, they looked like the devil's incarnate--in duplicate.

The battle lasted for twenty horrifying minutes, with terrible injuries being inflicted on both animals. The whole time, Dave laid low hoping the ordeal would soon end.

When the devils finished their two-moose war, one limped away. For several hundred feet in every direction, it looked as if a cyclone had touched down. Small trees had been knocked down, stumps were uprooted, and limbs and debris were scattered everywhere in the snow. The old bull moose had once again defeated a young challenger. He quickly trotted off to claim the cow that was waiting in the nearby brush.

Dave knew he had just witnessed the brutal, ugly side of nature. Watching the battle had been so terrifying, he didn't even notice when the gun loosened its grasp and slipped from his lip. His heavy breathing during the battle had completely defrosted the barrel.

The fierce performance by the very animal Dave was hunting left an unforgettable impression of just how violent the creature could be. He didn't need any more excitement for that day, so Dave left the area to return home. Walking along the trail, Dave made the decision he'd spend more time with experienced hunters who knew all about the savage creature called moose. He thought Charlie Minaker might be a good one to talk to.

An experienced hunter, Charlie Minaker had tracked a moose for two miles while hiking up snow-covered hills through thick timber and heavy windfall. Finally, he was able to get a good shot and downed the animal. As daylight was dwindling he hurriedly field dressed it, then prepared an eighty pound ham to be packed out. Charlie was a tree faller and had worked in the woods all his life, so he was still in pretty good shape at fifty-five years old. Still, the chore of packing the meat proved difficult for him, as it would for a man half his age. His plan was to recruit some help and return the next morning for the meat.

Twelve hours later, Charlie, Dave, Gary, and four other packers arrived at the snow-packed trail leading to the carcass. The determined hikers fought their way over windfall, slick rocks and steep terrain, all the time knowing that the trip in would be nothing compared to the trip out. Two hours later, the men arrived at the location where Charlie had left the moose. They found only a large blood-stained area in the snow, but no moose.

The puzzled group looked for clues and it didn't take long to pin down the prime suspect--a larcenous grizzly bear. The perpetrator had left a clearly defined trail by dragging its prey a hundred feet away. There, they found a moose mound covered over with leaves, branches and dirt. Instantly the men felt uneasy, knowing the bear might still be in the area and return for its bounty. Gary made a decision to track it to make sure it wasn't in the immediate area, protecting its cache.

It was obvious that the bear had dug a shallow pit before burying the carcass, so getting the huge animal to level ground proved to be a real chore. Once accomplished, the men started to cut and bone the meat. Using snow to remove the dirt, the meat was cleaned and wrapped in plastic then stuffed into backpacks. Soon, Gary returned to help with the clean-up and loading, with the good news that the moose thief had left the area.

Each packer, weighted down with eighty extra pounds, started the long journey back to the road. The men worked their way through windfall and down steep, slippery grades. The moose meat venture turned into a chore of monumental proportions, and the seven worn-out packers were happy to arrive safely at the end of the trail.

Ironically, Bob and Mack were out road hunting the same day and had shot a large buck within minutes of leaving the house. The deer had been standing on a hill when it was shot, so after it was dressed out, the men took hold of the antlers and drug it down the slope and into the truck.

They drove a little further up the valley and soon Bob fired again at a large moose climbing a hill. The animal died instantly. When it fell, it continued to slide on down the hill toward the waiting vehicle. Bob and Mack gladly helped the moose the rest of the way by backing up to the hill and sliding it into the truck. Then they headed home for a convenient spot to clean and butcher the animals. The men had only been gone from home two hours.

The seven worn-out packers and would-be bear killers were appalled at the news of the easy hunt.

After resting up from the grueling pack trip, Dave determined that moose hunting would be more fun if it was done from a horse. So, in the late fall of 1966, Dave went on a moose hunting trip with the infamous old sourdough and early pioneer of the Anahim Lake region, Lester Dorsey. Mike Dorsey, Lester's son, accompanied Dave while making the hundred-mile trip to Lester's ranch.

The old Anahim homestead sat in some of the coldest country on the Chilcotin plateau. As Dave and Mike arrived late one evening, the temperature dipped well below zero. The old log cabin was a welcomed sight with its dimly lit rooms and smoke-puffing chimney. The aroma of venison stew filled the air, and Lester's cabin seemed to have a personality all its own. It resembled a pack rat's nest with volumes of clutter.

Lester was a likable old guy who appeared to be as tough as shoe leather. He was in a constant state of rolling or smoking a roll-your-own cigarette while busily moving about. His beat-up old hat gave the impression it was well used. If it could only talk, it would have quite a story to tell. Dave soon realized the Chilcotin sourdough was part of a lost breed.

After resting for the night, Mike and Dave enjoyed a hearty breakfast that Lester cooked for them. Then, they prepared for a day of moose hunting in sub-zero weather. Decked out in moose-hide chaps, wool-lined leather mittens, a toque, a down-filled vest, a down-filled jacket with kidney protectors, two pairs of wool socks in felt-lined boots, Dave could hardly walk, let alone climb up on a large horse. An inexperienced rider, Dave prayed for a real gentle horse. He surveyed Lester's stock, hoping to find just the right one. After making his choice, the three men saddled up and rode their mustangs toward a snow-covered meadow.

They suddenly became aware of how cold it was as they had difficulty breathing the frozen air, but they rode on. Soon, they decided to split up, hoping to increase their chances of seeing game.

Off on his own, Dave soon came across a small group of four moose. They spotted him too, and by the time he got the horse stopped, mittens off and gun pulled from the scabbard, the moose had already slipped into the jackpine. Dave was astounded at how quickly they moved through the thick timber. Tilting their heads back, they used their huge antlers to crash through branches in their way.

Continuing to hunt for another hour, Dave realized the crunchy snow sounds generated by the horse's hoofs were warning any game well in advance.

Returning to the small stream where the three men had split up, Dave could see several tracks. The moose had outsmarted the hunters by circling around them and had come to the stream to drink. They'd broken the ice on the stream, drank, then dripped water all over the area around the watering hole. Because of the cold temperature, the falling droplets had frozen as fast as they hit the ground and had created a very slippery surface. The horse's hoofs also had built-up ice, so when they met the icy surface, horse and rider went down.

Landing on icy snow, Dave managed to remain in the saddle. But the horse ended up landing on top of him. The stunned animal groaned with frustration at being up-ended while Dave groaned from the weight of the huge animal. The horse heaved forward several times, trying to lift itself while Dave lay helplessly pinned beneath. With the freezing temperature, Dave was already numb from head to toe so he didn't feel any pain. His main concern was the animal might break free and return to the cabin without him. He was determined to stay with the horse, no matter what. The thrashing continued for several minutes. Finally, Dave slipped out from under the upset animal. He held the reins tightly in his hands.

After some effort, the horse finally stood on all fours. Spooked and upset, the animal managed to step on Dave's feet several times as it pranced about. Dave didn't notice much pain, just a slight stinging sensation. Somehow, Dave managed to calm the animal, remount, and after a lot of persuasion, they headed back to the ranch.

Long after his return to Lester's cabin, when he thawed out a bit, Dave became aware of sore legs, feet, arms, and back. No longer numb, he felt like he'd been run over by a large truck.

It took several days for his pain to subside. Dave concluded that moose hunting was some of the hardest work a person could ever do. But even so, he also realized he'd had the experience of a lifetime, that of moose hunting with one of Anahim Lake's legendary characters. To him, the trip had been well worth it.

Hunting game continued to be important as it supplemented our food budget, and certain times of the year were devoted to that purpose. The men enjoyed hiking back into remote areas, so hunting for game sometimes became an excuse to get away and enjoy the outdoors.

On one trip, Bob, Gary and Dave hiked back into the Little Rainbow Mountains located between Anahim Lake and the Bella Coola Valley. It was a difficult area to get into, but once there, the scenery was spectacular. The Rainbows were famous for meadows carpeted with flowers and brilliantly colored peaks of eroded lava covered in vegetation. There were lush valleys where clear streams wound through bunch grass meadows. But most of all, the area was renown for its trophy bucks and moose.

While hiking the area, the men found old abandoned trapping trails littered over with downed timber. On this particular trip, they met up with Thomas Squinas and his wife, clearing trails for Thomas' guiding service.

Thomas was of the Ulkatcho Native people and had lived all his life in the area around Anahim Lake. He knew the Rainbow Mountains and surrounding area like the back of his hand. He'd trapped and hunted there all his life. Every summer Thomas' family made a trek to the lowlands of the Atnarko Valley to catch fish, pick berries and trade with their Nuxalk neighbors.

Dave instantly liked Thomas Squinas. He had a quiet strength and sense of humor that made him stand out even though he rarely went out of his way to attract attention to himself. Thomas loved to tell interesting stories and was a walking encyclopedia of knowledge regarding the area and the folklore around Anahim Lake.

One of his amazing stories was about his father, Domas Squinas, who'd been chief of the Ulkatcho people. The chief was out hunting for moose and managed to shoot a bull. The bull fell to the ground, but when the chief walked up to it, it suddenly raised up and charged him. Hunters familiar with moose know that a charging bull can be as deadly as a charging grizzly bear, and do just as much damage. The chief ran for a tree and climbed it, but the moose pushed it over knocking him to the ground. Then the moose stomped on the poor man, injuring his face and braking several ribs. Thomas' father later died from his injuries.

Thomas was well known in the remote outreaches of the Chilcotin Plateau. He maintained a fiercely independent and self-sufficient lifestyle--living in a large ranch house he'd built himself--where he and his wife raised a large family. His ranch supported over 500 cattle, 300 sheep, and 100 head of horse.

Thomas was a man of many talents. When people needed something of an extraordinary nature done, he was the one they called. At one time, wolves were ravaging both the wildlife and domestic stock throughout the countryside, and it was Thomas the authorities hired to reduce their numbers.

During the Second World War, Thomas guided a thousand infantrymen over wintry passes to Bella Coola on a training exercise.

A few years later, Thomas was asked to seek out a route for a road to be built through the wilderness by volunteer labor. Thomas had known Lige Gurr very well.

Meeting up with the Native wolf hunter was an experience Dave would never forget.

Bob, Gary and Dave started blazing a trail of their own into the Little Rainbow Mountains which were just before the larger range. They used a compass and took note of important landmarks around them. The country all looked the same, and the added precautions would prevent them from getting lost. Once a hiker became disoriented, he couldn't tell north from south. The men used surveyor's ribbon to mark trees while making their way into the back country. After hiking all day, they arrived at a large meadow where they made camp. A little lake lay off in the distance but they stayed clear of it because of the giant mosquitoes that infested the area.

Age, size, and experience seemed to play a vital role in the male pecking-order on camp trips. Bob, at 27-years-old, was an experienced hunter. He stood six feet two inches tall and had a husky build. Gary, at 23-years-old, was also an experienced hunter, stood six feet three inches tall, and had a slender build. Dave, at 23-years-old was the least experienced hunter. He stood five feet eleven inches tall and had a medium build. The two Shelton brothers had already designated Dave as the official camp cook.

The veteran hunters quickly instructed the camp cook to get things set up and start dinner while they hunted for game.

Later, when the brothers returned from their hunting trip, the food was all ready, and Dave informed them he wanted to take a look around for game. Bob and Gary noted the ample supply of firewood for the evening fire, and for the breakfast meal the next day. Then they gave Dave his last minute instructions.

"Take the compass with you," Gary said.

"I won't need it," Dave replied. "I'm just going to circle around the lake and check for any fresh sign."

"Take the compass," Gary warned again.

"Hell, Gary, there's only one lake here. I know I can find my way back from that." Dave walked off still grumbling to himself, wondering what the big deal was about the compass.

After an hour of walking, Dave arrived at the backside of the lake and found a timbered ridge that he started hiking up. It turned out to be higher than he anticipated, and while Dave watched for sign, he continually climbed higher and higher. Finally, he reached the top and peered out over the area below. He expected to look down on a little lake with two campers sitting around a campfire. Instead, what he saw was a series of four lakes running in a straight line. He'd climbed higher than he thought. Then Dave realized that the lakes all looked the same. He couldn't see anything that would identify which one was close to the camp, so he decided he better backtrack. Suddenly, he became disoriented. He wasn't sure which direction was which. Everything looked the same.

Making a quick decision, he headed for the lake he "guessed" was the right one. He hiked for an hour and finally came to a lake expecting to find the camp, but there was no camp. The sun was beginning to set and Dave felt a little nervous about being lost. He decided to fire a shot from his rifle hoping Bob and Gary would return a shot to identify their location. He fired a round and stood still waiting for the return shot.

Nothing.

Nervous, Dave walked on toward the second lake hoping he was heading in the right direction. Daylight was fading fast as night set in. He walked quickly trying to beat the darkness. When he finally reached the second lake, there still was no camp. He fired another round and noticed a bright flash from the end of the barrel as darkness took over. He listened for a return shot.

Still nothing. The only sound Dave could hear was the rapid beating inside his chest.

He started hiking toward the third lake at a much faster pace. The terrain was rough and the fear of running into a bear made the hair on the back of his neck stand straight up. By now, he was down to three bullets.

When Dave approached the third lake that looked just like the two previous lakes, much to his relief, off in the distance he could see a campfire. He walked swiftly toward the two campers who sat leisurely enjoying the night air. They didn't appear too concerned about anything.

"Hey, didn't you hear my shots?" Dave yelled, breathing heavily as he entered camp.

"Yeah," Bob replied. "We heard them."

"Then why didn't you return a shot?" Dave asked.

"We knew you were heading in the right direction from the sound of the shots," Bob said.

"Yeah, but I didn't know that I was heading in the right direction," Dave said in an angry tone. Then he asked once more, "Why didn't you fire a shot?"

"Because," Gary said slowly, "You needed to learn a lesson."

Dave stood with his jaws locked tight. The two brothers sat staring at him.

There are moments in everyone's life when reality reaches out and says, "You made a mistake." This was one of those moments for Dave.

Like it or not, a lesson had been learned, a valuable one. Staring into the fire and feeling a bit foolish, Dave pictured a dictionary in his hands. He knew if he looked in the dictionary under DUMB PILGRIM he would see a picture of himself with a confused look on his face. He also knew that if he turned the page of that same dictionary, he would find a picture of Bob and Gary under SCHOLARS OF DUMB PILGRIMS, appearing very impressed by their own infinite wisdom. But, no matter what, he was safe and back at camp. He could deal with his mistake.

The next morning, the two brothers hunted for game while the camp cook finished breakfast and cleaned up. Later, it was decided by all they should hike back out because the weather was much too warm and most game would be higher up. The threesome started their long hike along the marked trail.

"We'll have to ration our water while hiking out," Gary said.

It was difficult hiking with only small amounts of water because the sun was constantly bearing down on them. Packing camp gear and rifles made it all the more difficult. They made a few stops to rest along the way and took only small sips of water, not wanting to use up their precious supply. Dave seemed remarkably happy while hiking out and had a constant grin on his face.

"You need water?" Gary yelled back to Dave.

"No, I'm fine."

They followed the survey ribbon while their pace gradually slowed down and they stopped more frequently to rest. Bob and Gary sipped small amounts of water but Dave sipped even less. He still supported a cunning grin.

When they neared the end of the journey, all three were sweating like horses. They had used up all their water and had to finish the rest of the trip with very dry mouths. Finally, a quarter mile from the parked truck, Dave veered off the trail and headed down a ravine toward a stream.

"Where are you going?" Bob asked.

"Well, it's like this," Dave said, "I figured that we'd be pretty thirsty by the time we hiked out, so I stashed some beer in the stream just below here."

"You did not," Bob said.

"You couldn't have," Gary said.

Dave didn't say another word. He quickly headed down the hill.

Bob and Gary discussed the possibility of beer being stashed in the creek. They finally decided that Dave was just trying to trick them and they weren't going to fall for it.

"We're hiking on out," Gary yelled to Dave who was no longer in sight.

Further down the trail Bob and Gary stopped.

"You don't think he really has beer in that stream do you?" Bob asked, beads of sweat pouring from his face.

"Nah," Gary said through parched dry lips.

They walked on a little further. Finally, their curiosity and thirst got the best of them so they turned back to find Dave.

"If he doesn't have beer, I'll kill him," Bob complained.

Eventually, the two hot and sweaty hikers caught up to Dave's trail. They started down it still grumbling about what they were going to do to Dave for tricking them. When they finally arrived at the stream, they stood staring at the unbelievable sight before them.

Leaning back on a large moss-covered rock, Dave had removed his boots, rolled up his pant legs and was now soaking his tired feet in the cool mountain stream. The relaxed expression on his face seemed to beam with contentment. His eyes were closed and in his hand was a bottle. It was an icy, cold bottle of beer.

"You dirty dog," Bob yelled.

Dave didn't move.

"OK," Gary said, getting impatient with the sight before him, "Where's the beer?"

Dave opened his eyes, slowly raised up and took a sip of beer, letting some trickle down his chin.

"Why didn't you tell us you brought beer?" Gary asked.

Bob joined in, "Yeah, why didn't you tell us you brought beer?"

Dave slowly took another sip then said, "You guys needed to learn a lesson."

"Oh yeah," Bob said.

"What's the lesson?" Gary asked.

"From now on, if you want a camp cook, you better bring Johnny along," Dave informed them.

Bob and Gary looked at each other.

"OK," they both agreed.

Dave reached into the stream and pulled out two cold bottles of beer. The two brothers guzzled them down while Dave leaned back in his resting place. He thought about that dictionary. Under JUSTICE FOR ALL he imagined a picture of Bob, Gary and himself holding up a beer and saying, "Cheers".

9

HARD TIME PARTIES

During the early days of logging, British Columbia, Alaska, Washington, Oregon, and northern California were referred to as the "Big Woods". The Big Woods provided the North American Continent with its first industry and the greatest logging operations the world has ever known.

The Big Woods had a certain majestic beauty that was captivating. For those working within its boundaries, the serenity of the woods could also be very dangerous. Each day brought new hazards, and it took a special breed of man just to wear the logger's boots.

Dave enjoyed working in the woods of the Pacific Northwest. He also relished hearing stories of earlier times when loggers used archaic methods to topple giant trees.

Coastal Cedars had a wide, flared base and presented a unique problem for early lumberjacks. The logger needed to be high off the ground where the trunk tapered off, so he could make a deep undercut. One of the most unusual but practical devices ever developed was the springboard. The wooden slat, eight inches wide and five feet long, had iron tips. The board was light enough to carry but strong enough to support a logger's weight. The iron tips were designed to grip the wood so a logger could "jump" the board sidewise without dislodging it from a chopped boardhole. While he was chopping the undercut with an ax, the logger's life literally rested on his springboard.

Cedars weren't the only problem. There were times when handloggers used springboards on other trees to set the direction the tree would fall on steep side hills. At times like this, the logger balanced out over a cliff.

To use his springboard, the logger first formed a deep wide notch in a tree. This was the boardhole. Into the boardhole went the springboard. The logger climbed onto the springboard, hooked the toe of one boot under the board, and jumped it around the tree to just the right spot.

Sometimes the logger had to go up two or three boards high. To accomplish this, he stood on the first springboard and chopped another boardhole at waist level. Then he inserted the second board and climbed up on it. Standing there, he chopped the third hole, then, reaching down with his ax, he lifted the first board up and placed it in the boardhole. Standing three boards high, while swinging the long-handled falling ax, the logger relied on his calked boots for safe footing.

Throughout the Valley, old cedar stumps with springboard holes, revealed the difficulty of falling large trees during an earlier age.

Dave thought that being part of the Pacific Northwest with its incredible logging history was the most adventuresome thing he'd ever done. He stood in awe of the loggers that came before with their old-time methods, and the men that he now worked with using more modern techniques. Dave was proud just to wear the logger's boots.

Dave had worked for Crown Zellerbach as a logger for one year. As a newcomer to the Logging Industry, he felt he'd done well just to survive, but it hadn't been easy. Perhaps his encounter with the stick to the face, early on, left a lucid impression of just how lethal working in the woods could be. That, and the every-day stories of injuries only heightened that awareness. There were haunting memories of men who'd been killed while working in the woods; with names like Teddy Celnes, Oli Nickoli, Edgar Saunders, Olaf Nygaard, Alvin Odegaard, Patrick Jack, Malfred Nygaard, and Barry Mecham.

Dave had been tutored by some of the best woodsmen who'd ever lived. He'd learned the safe way to set chokers on steep side hills while a tower operator yarded the logs with heavy cables to a cold deck pile. He knew the importance of maintaining a constant awareness of the Whistle Punk who gave the different signals correlating the activities between the tower and the men. This was very important because the tower operator never had the men in sight while releasing and pulling the cables.

Dave had also learned to work with a shovel operator while setting 70-pound tongs during a truck loading operation.

When Dave became Headloader, it was because his predecessor, Jimmy Jack, born and raised in the Valley, was killed in a logging accident. The Native man had been moonlighting on the weekends working for a gyppo logger in the Necleetsconnay Valley. Jimmy was an excellent worker, and had many years of work experience in the woods. His life had been instantly snuffed out when a cold deck pile accidentally rolled on him, crushing him beyond recognition.

Dave was saddened to hear about the horrible accident. Then, a short time later, another logger was killed.

Nels Brekke had worked in the logging industry all his life. He was a very competent, safety minded employee who looked out for others as well as himself. He came from a family of loggers who'd spent thousands of hours in the woods. When Dave worked with Nels on a previous work site, Nels was the whistle punk and Dave literally placed his life in his hands while they worked.

At the time Nels was killed, he was still working as a whistle punk. He was killed in a bizarre accident when a sapling struck him in the back of the head. Fellow workers were terribly saddened at the loss of Nels Brekke.

As Headloader, Dave stood on a platform atop truck cabs and stamped large logs. This form of identification showed ownership once the log was boomed up in the inlet and transported to Vancouver. It was also his job to release the tongs that hauled the logs from the woods to the top of the truck.

On one occasion, Dave was standing on a truck load of logs and accidentally lost his footing when he released the tongs. The drop to the ground was about thirty feet so he instinctively reached for the line from the shovel. Ken Stranaghan, the shovel operator, quickly took up the slack on the line causing Dave to go from horizontal to vertical in a split second. Anyone watching would have thought it was a practiced, well-choreographed move.

Dave marveled at the expertise of the loggers around him. They manipulated heavy equipment and huge logs with a certain type of skill that only comes after countless years of experience.

One work day, Dave watched as Doug Gurr operated a grapple. A large tree that he wanted to load still had branches on it. Doug stood the tree on end with the grapple hook. While the tree was balanced in an upright position, he eased up on the hydraulic pressure. This allowed the grapple hook to slide down the log, trimming it of the branches as it fell. When the hook neared the base of the log, Doug increased the hydraulic pressure and the enormous jaws tightened around the log. In one swift movement, Doug picked the log up and loaded it onto the logging truck. He accomplished the task as if he were playing with a match stick. Still grinning from ear to ear, Doug knew this technique was a simple way to eliminate a problem. To Dave, it was an incredible feat.

From a safe distance, Dave watched as fallers fell huge trees with giant gear-driven chain saws. It was their job to fall the gigantic trees to precise locations, and they did it with a certain skill that commanded respect. Once trees were down, they were scaled and bucked at the proper length. Measurements were recorded in a book which not only determined wages, but also kept an accurate account of how much timber had been fallen. Next, the buckers moved in with smaller chain saws and removed all the branches. Then chokers were set, logs were moved and trucks were loaded.

For decades the logging industry had furnished incomes to families. But now, world economies were slowing down and there was less demand for lumber.

As a result of the poor economy, Crown Zellerbach started cutting its work force. Dave was laid off, but soon landed a job working for Northcop Sawmill. Fortunately, the mill had several lumber contracts still pending, and they needed a Tail Sawyer. The prospects of wintertime employment made us both very happy, even if it turned into part time work due to freeze up.

It was during this same time I learned I was expecting another baby. The thought of being pregnant again, so soon, was a little overwhelming as baby Pam was only six months old.

Our poor old GMC pickup truck was slowly falling apart. The trip across the Chilcotin had taken its toll. Without the necessary funds to repair the deterioration process that was taking place, it was just a matter of time until the once dependable truck became nonfunctional. Just getting it to start was a major ordeal.

My sister Phyllis and I watched as Dave performed his ritual of getting the truck started. First, he turned the ignition key on and pumped the gas pedal. Next he walked to the front of the truck, opened the hood, and climbed up on the bumper. Reaching over the engine, he placed a screw driver next to the worn out solenoid shorting out the system, and causing the starter to respond with a spark to the engine. While the engine struggled to keep running, Dave hurriedly climbed down, shut the hood with a loud bang, then ran around to the driver's door. Climbing in the cab, he quickly pumped the gas pedal so the engine wouldn't die.

Feeling confident the truck would remain running, he attempted to close the door that had a worn out latch. SLAM...SLAM...SLAM. The deafening noise echoed through the close quarters of the cab and the frame of the broken side mirror wobbled with each attempt.

Finally, the door latched and Dave furiously pumped on the gas pedal to keep the engine running. His composure was still intact at this point, but when he placed the transmission in gear and the engine died, he lost it. Out came the cuss words wrought with emotion revealing his frustration. And the whole process started all over again.

We watched as the madman raced around in front of the truck, opened the hood, by-passed the solenoid, closed the hood, jumped in the cab, pumped the gas pedal, tried to shut the door, SLAM...SLAM...SLAM, feverishly pumped the gas pedal for several minutes and placed the transmission in gear. We all sat motionless when the engine died for the second time. By then Dave was so furious he couldn't speak.

Once again Dave opened the hood, by-passed the solenoid, closed the hood, jumped in the cab, pumped the gas pedal, tried to shut the door, SLAM...SLAM...SLAM, and more gas pumping, then he placed it in gear. On his third attempt he gave the engine so much gas it couldn't possibly stall. Holding on for dear life, we were cruelly tossed about while exiting our bumpy driveway in record speed.

Then, the loose latch on the glove compartment released and all it's contents flew out on the floor. After replacing everything, Dave started slamming the glove box door trying to get it to latch. SLAM...SLAM...SLAM.

By then, our minds were so distraught from all the commotion, we couldn't remember where we were going as we started down the road.

The hard times of the previous winter seemed somehow diminished by the possibility of severe economic problems facing the Valley. It was during these bleak uncertain times that a miraculous thing happened. It happened quite by accident because it centered around a chance meeting of some new arrivals to the Valley. Their names were Graham and Angela Hall.

Graham and Angela had recently married in Vancouver, then moved to Bella Coola to start a new life. They had a ready-made family because Angela had been previously married and had five children: Chelle' ten-years-old, the twins Janet and Jenny nine-years-old, Victor six-years-old, and Billy five-years-old. Angela was from California, and Graham had been born and raised in Canada.

Graham Hall was a fisherman. And fishing wasn't just another "hobby" to Graham, because a hobby would've been done in his "spare time". Being an avid fisherman was only one of his many achievements. Most importantly, he had the ability to be a good step-father to five children. He also had a Third Degree Black Belt in Judo, was a Martial Arts instructor, wood craftsman, master carpenter, and champion chess player. Angela had been a professional singer as well as dance instructor, loved ballroom dancing and could execute any dance step with grace and skill. The one thing that stood out even more than the couple's many talents was their talent for having fun.

Halloween was a special event to both Graham and Angela. It was at a big Halloween party in

Vancouver where they had met. When Graham and his date arrived at the party, Angela was doing a hula accompanied by a band playing and chanting a Hawaiian tune; she had near-waist length flowing hair, and was wearing a grass skirt, halter, and a flower lei. Graham, handsome and dignified in a dark blue suit, caught her glance. All during the night their eyes met, but not a word was spoken. After Angela went home from the party she was startled by a knock on her door. It was Graham. What started out as an instant attraction quickly ignited, and by Christmas they announced their wedding plans to their shocked and disbelieving friends and relatives. It was a pretty quick decision for two people who had vowed never to marry again.

It was mid-October of 1966 when we received an invitation from Angela to attend a Halloween party that she and her sister Star were planning. Star, also a transplant to the Valley, was a talented pianist, thespian and dancer. Good news for me, both Star and Angela wore makeup.

We were happy to accept the invitation. Both Dave and I agreed we really wanted to get to know the Hall family. It didn't take us long to plan our costumes. Dave would go as a cowboy, and I would be a logger dressed in a cruising vest and hard hat. Being almost six months pregnant, I could hide my belly with a long flannel shirt.

It was a very interesting group that attended the Halloween party. Most of them we'd never met, and there were several the Hall's hadn't met before either. Several folks just showed up, invited or not. As we mingled and got to know one another, it became very obvious that we all came from different backgrounds. We did, however, have one important thing in common. We loved to have fun.

"Who is that strange man, dressed like a woman, the one who keeps flirting with me?" Dave asked as he leaned toward me.

"That's Reverend Mike Bolger from the United Church," I replied.

"Is he married?" Dave asked suspiciously.

"Yes," I whispered, and pointed at the red-faced woman, hiding in the corner.

"Oh," Dave said and relaxed a bit. By that time, Reverend Bolger and Star's husband Cecil, who was dressed in a Dracula costume, were doing some fine dancing to a lively rock-and-roll tune.

We also met Willie and Colleen Phillips. Willie was the son of Panhandle Phillips, one of Anahim Lake's early pioneers and cattle rancher. Willie came dressed as a Manchurian, and Colleen was hilarious in her Mexican outfit that was stuffed with a large pillow.

The idea of a costume party had really caught on. I remember Marge and Cyril Christensen came as a Neanderthal couple with furs covering their bodies, and bones in their hair. Gerald Saugstad was in a baseball uniform, Gunde Frostrup was dressed in authentic Arab garb, Star was in a form-fitting cat-woman outfit, Graham appropriately dressed as a Samurai warrior, and Angela as a geisha.

Everywhere you looked in the crowded room was another example of the ingenuity going into a costume. That was no small feat in Bella Coola because no one sold ready-made costumes.

What wonderful food there was at the party. Graham caught and baked a twenty-five pound Coho. There were salads, vegetables, homemade

145

rolls, and desserts. Also potato chips and dip, a real treat, because they certainly weren't on our grocery budget. A box of potato chips at the Co-op cost as much as five dollars.

We talked, visited, laughed, and ate. We all agreed we should have another party real soon, so Dave and I offered to host the next one. We explained that we didn't have the best of living conditions. We had no running water or electricity, and even our bathroom facilities were primitive. We had nothing fancy in the way of dishes or clothes to wear, so Dave and I made a quick decision and announced that we'd be hosting a Hobo Party. Each person was to bring their own tin can to eat out of, and a vegetable to go into the stew pot. Hobo attire was a must and if anyone dressed too nicely, heaven help them!

Everyone eagerly agreed to attend the Hobo Party dressed like a bum.

And so the Hard Time Parties were born. Born in fun and born in spite of the looming financial problems facing the Valley.

We invited the rest of my family to the Hobo Party and they all fit right in with the fun-loving newly formed group. We cooked a big pot of venison stew, adding each of the vegetables as guests arrived at our humble abode. We sat in a circle on the floor in the living room, dressed in rags while eating out of tin cans. Napkins were small sheets of toilet paper and were considered a rare commodity by those who'd become accustomed to last year's Simpson-Sears catalog. Reverend Bolger seemed to know all about Hobo's. He had his own set of hobo utensils that were easily carried in a pocket. Later that evening, we played some pretty silly games in that dimly-lit room that revealed happy, tramp-like, laughing faces.

I once asked my brother Gary if he remembered the first time he met Graham Hall.

He responded, "Yes, it was at a Hobo Party at your house. We were all dressed like tramps and we played a silly game called Fox and Hunter."

I remembered that game. A table was placed in the middle of the room. The hunter was selected (Gary) and a blindfold was placed over his eyes. Next, a fox was selected (Graham) and he also received a blindfold. The hunter didn't know who the fox was, and the objective of the game was to discover the identity of the fox once the fox was caught. As the two players moved clumsily around the table while blindfolded, the hunter pursued the fox. When the fox felt or heard the hunter coming, he escaped around the table in the opposite direction. Neither one could see anything and the rest of us sat laughing as one pursued and the other escaped. Finally, the hunter caught his prey and had to identify who it was. The fox, of course, was not allowed to speak. The only way the hunter could identify the fox was to feel him, all over, while trying to touch something that would give a clue. Gary ran his hands over Graham's face while touching his nose, his mouth, and his neck. Then he worked his way down to his arms and felt his muscles. A few obscene remarks and gestures were added by both and we all laughed at their antics.

"Yes," Gary said, "I remember being introduced to Graham Hall and the next thing I knew I was running my hands all over his body. How could I forget that?"

With such an intimate meeting, it was inevitable that a life-long friendship was sparked, and that certainly was the case for the two men. Angela and Sandy didn't have to play a silly game to establish their friendship, and the two couples became very good friends.

While the Hard Time Parties continued, holidays and birthdays took on a special meaning as we planned parties around hard times and what they brought. Presents were handmade or hand-me-downs. We used the same birthday card over and over and the last recipient was in charge of passing the card on for the next birthday. The same card was also used for anniversaries so it became well worn. We cooked dishes from whatever we had. Because everyone stored oatmeal, powdered milk, potatoes, carrots, and flour, we always had lots of dishes made from those ingredients. Meat dishes were moose, venison, or fish. We set up a commodity exchange. Anything that was in abundance in one household could be exchanged for something someone else had lots of. For example: Angela was in need of hand lotion and I needed soap. I had extra lotion because Dave's mother had given us a large supply before our departure from California. We gladly exchanged supplies.

The next Hard Time Party took place at my Mom and Dad's place. Instead of having it in their small cabin, the party was held at the Robin's Nest Cafe where they worked as managers. My mother was well-known for her great cooking, and the meal she prepared was wonderful. We all felt like we'd dined at an exquisite restaurant.

With so little entertainment available, it was the inherent nature of our group to be creative, to come up with a unique game for each party, one that could be played by all. We learned to play Help Your Neighbor which required everyone to sit in a large circle. Someone was selected to stand in the middle and walk around the circle until they pointed at someone then yelled out the name of an animal. If the animal was an elephant, the person had to jump up and make a trunk-like formation with their arms while their two adjacent neighbors had to jump up and form ears for the elephant's head. Who ever messed up and didn't complete their part of the elephant became the one in the middle. If bird was yelled out the middle person made a beak-like form while the two on each side flapped wings.

Each animal had an assigned form that had to be memorized and played out in a second's notice. Usually the person in the middle yelled the animal name so loudly and so fast it was hard to think or do anything. It was also quite difficult to remember what ear, leg or wing went with which animal, and the results were hilarious. We watched elephant trunks with one flapping wing and bird beaks with elephant ears as game players tried to respond accurately. There were other animals to be acted out like cat, dog, horse, cow, penguin, and bear.

We played another game called Gossip. It was one of our favorites because those living in a small community, with little entertainment, know all too well that gossip is a very realistic part of everyday activities. The idea was to whisper a made-up story that was quite detailed and lengthy. One person would repeat it to another as it progressed around the room. At the end of the circle, the person receiving the last of the gossip would repeat what they had heard. Most often, it wasn't anything like the original story and it was pretty funny to see how many different twists and turns a story could take, just like real gossip.

My father was known for his artistic talents and drew wonderful caricatures. One of the games he invented was to give each person a three-way folded paper with instructions to draw a head, fold the paper over, then pass it to the next person who drew a body, without seeing the head it was to match. The third person drew the legs and feet without seeing the body or head. There were several masterpieces being worked on at a time, and when we opened the folds out, we could admire the hilarious art work.

Most evenings were finished off with a great egg rolling event, on the floor, using spoons.

After one party, Dave, Graham and Cecil planned a deer hunting trip to the upper Valley. While there, they came across a herd of deer moving slowly up a hill. Dave and Graham were to flush the deer back down the hill by moving around them and herding them toward Cecil who would be waiting. All Cecil had to do was shoot the game as it came toward him.

Graham and Dave quickly started their ascent up the snow-covered hill. They climbed for quite a ways, then waved to each other indicating they knew each other's position, and were ready to move the animals back the other way. As soon as they flushed the herd, the deer ran down the hill just like they were suppose to. Immediately, they heard a volley of shots as Cecil responded to the charging game.

Suddenly a bullet hit the tree above Graham, and he dove behind a rock. Dave started whistling and waving to indicate their location. A bullet sped passed his head and he dove for a rock. The two men were shocked and afraid to move from the protective rocks. They whistled once more and more shots rang out.

"I think he's trying to kill us," Graham yelled to Dave as a bullet ricocheted above him.

Finally, when it became quiet once more, they stood up. Seeing that Cecil was out of ammunition, the two angry men stormed down the hill. Graham wanted to kill his brother-in-law on the spot for the bullet that almost hit him in the head. When everyone settled down a bit, it became obvious that Cecil had displayed a bad case of Buck Fever. He'd gotten so excited at the sight of game, he started shooting at any sound or any movement. The sad part was, Cecil hadn't shot one deer, but had almost downed his two hunting partners. Graham and Dave vowed never to hunt with Cecil again.

Graham and Angela soon came to our house for a visit. We had so much fun telling humorous stories and entertaining ourselves we didn't notice the falling snow accumulating outside. Graham finally went out to start his vehicle and realized we were snowed in. Neither of our vehicles could get out of the long driveway now buried in snow.

There was nothing we could do, so we decided to play some games and make snow ice cream. The Hall children had never seen snow ice cream before and they thought it was a pretty crazy idea. We gathered fluffy, white snow in a large pan. Then we mixed can milk, sugar and vanilla, and poured the mixture over the snow until it resembled the same consistency as real ice cream. Everyone enjoyed the dessert so much, we decided to make it again the next day. This time we used maple flavoring instead of vanilla and added some chopped nuts.

Being unprepared for company, the only meat we had on hand was some ooligans that someone had given to us when they cleaned out their freezer. And there were hundreds of them. The ooligans resembled smelt, and were very rich with a high oil content.

Anything with water in it froze solid, including our plumbing, so it was necessary to go outside to use the fresh air facilities. Dave came up with a plan. The front yard was designated as the "clean snow" area, for making snow ice cream. The back yard was to be used for toilet facilities, and soon everyone made their own snow trail to a private spot. The winter wonderland in the back yard soon took on a road map appearance with nine different trails leading into the trees.

While the snow continued to fall, we continued to eat ooligans and snow ice cream for three days. Before long, the "frizzles" struck with a vengeance and all nine of us were hit with it. The end result was pure havoc as snow trails lost direction and desperation led the way.

From the onslaught, Dave warned that no one was to use the frozen indoor facility, *no matter what.* But sometime during the third night of our captivity, a desperate ooligan eater, suffering from distress, sneaked in and used the toilet rather than braving the sub-zero temperatures outside. The upset Dave conducted a thorough investigation of the "inside job," but the guilty culprit remained undetected. It was probably for the best--they might have been tarred and feathered, or at least rolled in ooligan grease.

By the end of the three days, we were all very happy to depart each other's miserable company.

Later, when Graham and Dave finally bagged a deer on their own, Angela and I decided to help with the butchering process. We also decided that our house, with the big kitchen, would be the best place to work. Angela and I had always found butchering a little morbid, requiring a week just to forget the gruesome task before we could eat any of the meat. Not this time. We were so hungry for something that resembled beef and something that didn't have gills, we quickly cut away a rump roast and placed it in the oven. As soon as the meat was packaged, we enjoyed a wonderful venison roast dinner with mashed potatoes and gravy.

In December, the Hard Time Christmas party was at our house. Dave wore a Santa Claus suit that he'd borrowed and handed out gifts to the kids. Everyone had worked hard on handmade gifts for the children. It was fun to watch baby Pam, almost a year old, enjoy her first Christmas. She had been given the nickname Skookie, a derivative of Skookum, the Norwegian term for strong.

That Christmas we received a package from Dave's mother in California. It had taken two weeks just to reach us. In the package were two white sweat shirts and a small package with a note addressed to both of us. The note said: Not to be opened until you're alone.

Dave and I couldn't imagine what was in the package, and we guessed all kinds of strange things before we finally opened it. What a surprise. It was a package of the best chocolate bridge mix available in the States. Our Christmas was complete. We feasted on each delectable morsel.

Dave and I were committed that before our next baby was born, we would have electricity. We saved every cent we could toward that goal, and it was a very special day when we achieved it. This meant we could use the old wringer washer that came with the house to wash clothes and diapers. We performed a little ceremony and gladly placed our scrub board to rest.

We still had to haul water from the Snootli Creek, so we made another vow that by next summer, we would have running water in the house.

We were still adjusting to the smallness of the community. You realize how small a community is when you decide to miss church one Sunday and end up receiving a get well card from the whole congregation; or, a call to a wrong number ends up in a long conversation anyway; and, you know who is going where just by watching out your front window because there is only one road. In a small community like Bella Coola, drivers didn't even use their turn signals. Why should they? Everyone knew where they were going. At times, the community seemed a little too small.

One evening, Dave and I wanted to watch a western movie at the old theater house in town. The small building that housed the theater needed many repairs. It was only open part time and showed movies that were quite old. To get a good seat, we always arrived early, but on this particular evening, we were late. The place was packed. We couldn't find any place to sit in the darkened room. Finally, the screen reflected more light and we saw three vacant seats in the second row from the front.

154

Our two silhouettes formed outlines on the illuminated screen while we squeezed down the narrow aisle; one of us thin and the other very pregnant. Finally, Dave sat down and I took the seat next to him. When my weight was evenly distributed on the old chair, it suddenly gave way and I hit the floor with a bang. The loud noise it created could be heard clear across the Chilcotin.

Shocked, Dave looked down on me. I was nestled between the arm rests, sitting on the floor, and I could hear whispering and giggles in the rows behind us. Dave stood up and tried to lift me by pulling on my arms, but it didn't do any good.

"I don't care how you do it, but you've got to get up," Dave whispered.

I managed to pull my legs up, giving me some leverage, and as Dave pulled, I pushed with everything I could muster up. Finally, my round silhouette blocked the screen once more and I heard many murmurings behind us. Dave moved over quickly to the next seat and I took over his. It was several minutes before either of us could concentrate on the movie in front of us.

During one of the shoot-outs with cowboys and Indians, we realized that the occupants of the first half of the theater were all Natives and they were cheering for the Indians in the movie. Back in the rear of the theater, we heard other locals cheering whenever the soldiers charged. We felt like fish out of water! When the movie was finally over, the lights came on and people began to walk toward the only exit.

"Are you ready to go?" Dave asked, staring straight ahead, numbed by the whole experience.

"Sure," I said, "Just as soon as everyone has left."

Fortunately, the collapsed seat only bruised my pride, and nothing else. But it was a long time before we attended another movie.

Sometime later, we enjoyed a Hard Time Birthday Party when Angela presented "This is Your Life" to her sister Star. Each of us had a role of a long lost relative or friend to play. We gave little "remember when" speeches that Angela had written out for us. Of course we got to dress accordingly, depending on who we represented, a man or a woman. Dave got to wear a tutu representing an old dance instructor while Graham wore a wig and scarf depicting an old friend. We learned a great deal about Star at the party and got to enjoy some of Angela's wonderful cooking.

Next, it was Reverend Bolger's turn to host a Hard Time Party. We were very excited because rumor had it we would be playing a new and exciting game.

When Dave and I prepared to leave for the party, I had one small dilemma: no underwear. My Simpson-Sears order had been lost right when I needed it most, and the old thread-bare panties, washed many times on the scrub board, simply gave out.

"I don't know what I'm going to do about underpants," I complained.

"Wear a pair of mine," Dave suggested.

"Oh, sure. I can just see me in Fruit-of-the-Loom."

"Well, at least there's an opening in the front. It will give you a little extra room for your tummy," Dave said as he laid a pair out on the bed. "Just wear them, no one will ever know."

I reluctantly put them on, and we both had a good laugh at how funny a pregnant woman looked in men's underwear.

"OK, you promise to never tell anyone? I'd die of embarrassment if you did," I warned.

"I promise," Dave said with a little gleam in his eye.

"If I'm rendered unconscious or go into labor, make sure I'm not wearing men's underwear when I go to the hospital, OK?"

Dave laughed but agreed to remove them if anything unforeseen happened. We left for the party.

Reverend Bolger and his wife Lillian had a lovely home in Bella Coola. They immediately made everyone feel welcome and it was good to see the hard time crew once again.

Lillian was extremely excited about the new game she'd seen on television while visiting in Vancouver. She happily announced that we would be playing "The Newly Wed Game". It sounded like fun.

Three couples volunteered to go first. Dave and I were one of the three. The men were sent out of the room while the women were asked questions. We wrote our answers down on paper and were suppose to predict what our husband would respond to the same question.

The first question: "Where will your husband say you went on your first date?"

This was easy. I wrote down: New Year's Eve Dance.

Second question: "What will your husband say is the one thing you would change about him, if you could?"

This one was easy, too. I wrote down: Stop Cussing.

Third question: "If your husband rated your cooking, would it be fair, good, or excellent?"

I hesitated for a moment then spelled out: Good.

Then the final question: "What is the one thing your husband knows he should never reveal about you?"

My whole body froze. Slowly, I looked across the room at our many friends and relatives. I rolled my eyes and looked toward the ceiling then down at my paper. I could just hear Dave saying, "Oh, she wears men's underwear." My face turned red at the thought. By then, everyone was staring at me while they waited, so I quickly wrote down: I Snore.

When the men returned to the room, I shot a desperate glance toward Dave that told him we had a problem. I hoped he would read my mind: "Don't you dare."

Dave looked puzzled as he sat down at the table across from me. In his mind he said: "What's wrong?"

I returned a look that said: "You promised," and I gave him the evil eye.

By this time, Dave was a little nervous and very confused.

"Dave," Lillian said, "What was the first date you and Caroline went on?"

Dave was afraid to speak. Finally he asked, "Was it a New Year's Eve Dance?" And his mind said, "What's so bad about that?"

I gave him a mind answer that said, "Just wait." Then I read my answer.

Next, Lillian asked what I would change about him.

Dave appeared nervous and I shot a mental note to him, "This isn't the problem, Dummy."

"She doesn't like me to cuss," Dave said cautiously.

I read my answer.

"How would you rate Caroline's cooking?" Lillian asked. "Fair, good or excellent?"

Dave thought he'd found the source of my agitation and a smile came to his face. In his mind he said, "OK, I'll be generous," so he responded: "good."

I stared at him with a hopeless expression as I read my answer.

I stared down at my paper as Lillian asked the final question, "What is the one thing you should never reveal about your wife?"

I slowly looked up and my mind said, "OK, Jocko, here it is."

Dave's face lit up as he finally made connection with the situation at hand, and he started to chuckle with delight. "Well now, let me see..."

I looked around the room at our many friends and relatives. Everyone seemed very intent on Dave's answer. They knew something was up.

"My wife..." Dave began, then laughed. "My wife..." (more laughter). "The truth is..." (Dave fought for composure). Finally, staring at the ceiling, Dave said, "My wife is so wonderful, I can't think of one thing."

With relief, I looked deep into his dark eyes and our minds met one more time. I said, "Pumpkin, you have a friend for life."

And he whispered back, "I know."

10

ROAD TRIPS

The Bella Coola Valley was famous for its stupendous mountains, lush forests, and great fishing; but what really set it apart from the rest of the world was the Hill, and the perseverance test crossing the Chilcotin. Weeding out many who failed, the Bella Coola Hill humbled even the most experienced traveler. For those who completed the journey and passed the test, there was a special degree, of sorts, one that deserved respect.

Visitors to the Valley were labeled as "courageous" and they were few in number. It took a special breed to complete the trip. One willing to suffer through anything for the sake of adventure.

A voyager of the Chilcotin was defined by one of two categories: Novice or Master.

A Novice managed to complete the 300 difficult miles, then in a moment of weakness, searched out an alternative route home. Often, a tenderfoot lost all credibility by departing out the inlet by ship.

Sometimes, a Novice made it as far as the Hill before turning back. Then there were those who refused to travel down the Hill in a moving vehicle. (There were countless stories of women walking the entire distance.)

By contrast, a Master voyager was someone who made the trip willingly, knowing what lay in store, and accepted the challenge. These adventuresome souls became excited just at the sight of the Bella Coola Hill. They savored the Chilcotin Road with its bump and grind torture test. (Secretly, they also loved roller coaster rides and white water rafting.)

The Bella Coola people liked to brag about their Hill. After all, it was unique. Throughout the seasons it presented many faces. Sometimes smooth and gentle, or covered over with an avalanche of snow or rock. At other times, it was rutted and broken away, or as icy as a skating rink. Only one thing remained constant about the Hill: it was always a challenge.

As risk-takers continued to conquer the grueling trail, there was an endless supply of road trip stories and Hill adventures being born.

Sandy Shelton saw the Chilcotin for the very first time when she and Gary moved to Bella Coola. She'd been raised in a suburb of Los Angeles, California, and her only requirement for her new home was good shopping. Gary assured her there'd be a place to shop in Bella Coola.

Traveling across the Chilcotin, Gary and Sandy made it past Alexis Creek without any problems. Then, their Ford van hit an uprooted cattle guard. The cattle guard had been damaged in a frost boil during spring breakup, and the protruding metal strips destroyed two tires. Eventually, they were towed back to Alexis Creek by a local man, and ended up spending the night at an old-fashioned hotel.

The old hotel provided the only pub for a hundred miles and catered to a steady stream of locals who regularly tipped the ol' sauce. It was

161

Saturday night and by 10:00 p.m., the place was hoppin' with a very rowdy crowd. Their loud rumblings could be heard, and felt, in every room of the hotel.

Gary made an inquiry about two new tires at a small garage across the street from the hotel. While there, he happened to notice a Native man hunched over and bleeding from a three inch gash on his cheek. Gary was an experienced fireman and knew first-aid. Instinctively, he responded to the man, fearing he might bleed to death right before his eyes. Gary volunteered to help, but the man refused.

"What happened?" Gary asked.

"Squaw hit me with broken beer bottle," the man replied. Then he leaned over a faucet and washed the gaping wound.

The next morning, Gary and Sandy were happy to depart from the old hotel. They'd had a restless night filled with fights, loud music, and no sleep.

Sandy couldn't help noticing how wild and untamed the country was in 1965. The further they traveled into the Chilcotin, the further back in time they went. As time travelers caught in a nostalgic yesteryear, they were now approaching the year 1865.

Just before Tatla Lake, the road became a quagmire of mud. Stopping, Gary took out an ax and cut down several jackpines, six-inches in diameter, to be used as punching. The punching would provide traction for the tires in the mud. After several miles of endless corduroy punching, they came across a new adversary--swollen streams flooding the road.

At last they reached Anahim Lake with its Native Reserve and a handful of white people. By then, Sandy was convinced she'd either left the planet earth or was a stranger on some lost continent.

The small general store at Anahim Lake was a combination store, post office and meeting place for locals. It sold food items five times the normal price, and had a strange assortment of animal furs, moccasins, axes, shovels, handy-man jacks, lanterns, candles, fishing gear, and endless rows of gumboots hanging from the rafters. Surprised by the unusual inventory, Sandy found herself wondering just what Gary's definition of "shopping" was.

Sandy finally arrived in the Bella Coola Valley. She soon discovered the Valley's beauty and found it very captivating. Still, she couldn't help feeling isolated. The remoteness of the Valley, along with its lack of conveniences and limited shopping, was quite a contrast from her former life.

Sandy's adjustment to the Valley was gradual. In time, she took part in such projects as clearing land, putting up fences and helping to build a cabin. Soon, everyone noticed that city-born Sandy had something special. She had grit.

When other family members started making the trip across the Chilcotin in 1966, it became a family procession with new arrivals and seasoned travelers meeting up at Williams Lake. For those who'd already experienced the Chilcotin test and passed, the journey back to civilization was worthwhile just to watch the unsuspecting faces of newcomers.

Bob and Shirley made their sojourn in a green 1940 Ford pickup with a homemade camper on back. They had four children and a

Saint Bernard pup that rode in the back. They traveled on used tires they'd purchased for $4 each.

Their vehicle problems started as early as Ashland, Oregon, when they lost two radiator hoses on a long descent of a grade. They continued on down the hill and coasted into a service station.

The service station attendant informed them he just so happened to have two hoses that would fit the old truck's flathead v-eight engine. He only charged them $1.50 for each hose, and they soon continued on their trip.

In a small Oregon town called Gold Hill, they experienced a broken rear axle. Again, they coasted into a small service station. Bob spoke to an attendant about locating a used axle, but the possibility of that happening in Gold Hill looked pretty bleak. Bob was certain they'd have to cancel their trip north. A twenty-five-year-old axle would be too difficult to locate.

The attendant gave them permission to spend the night at the service station. The next morning, Bob awoke and climbed out of the camper. He was startled to find a stranger sitting on a rock just a few feet from the truck.

"Well, it's about time you got up," the stranger said. "I've been waiting here quite awhile."

"What do you mean?" Bob asked.

"I understand you're looking for a rear axle," the man said.

"As a matter of fact I am, but how did you know that?"

"The service station attendant told me," he replied.

The man went on to explain that he was returning from a camping trip and had been away from home for several days. Back at his ranch was a barn, and in that barn was a 1940 Ford truck that was no longer in use.

By the time Shirley joined Bob outside, the men had already discussed how they were going to tow their truck out to the ranch twenty-five miles away, dismantle the old axle and put it in Bob's truck. Shirley was astounded.

Forty-five minutes later, the man pulled into the driveway of his ranch with the green truck in tow, plus the six stranded travelers and their dog. His wife looked a little surprised, but was soon cooking breakfast for everyone. The man's two sons went right to work removing the axle from the old truck that had been stored in the barn for who knows how long.

By noon, the axle was replaced and the Sheltons were ready to continue their trip.

"How much do I owe you?" Bob asked.

"You don't owe me one darn thing," the man said. "All I ask is, when you come back through sometime, be sure you stop for a visit."

The man put out his hand which Bob gladly shook. The Sheltons headed north once more.

Bob and Shirley finally arrived in Williams Lake and stopped at a park. Sometime later, Gary and Sandy met them at the park. The Bella Coola Sheltons had traveled fourteen hours through Chilcotin dust. Along for the ride were seasoned voyagers anxious to share the experience with the new arrivals; they were Phyllis, Johnny, Debbie and Clint.

A decision was made that Bob, Gary and Johnny would travel together in the truck while crossing the Chilcotin. The three women and six kids could all ride in the van, and the dog would ride in the camper.

In a decisive move, the men quickly pulled out ahead of the women. This meant the gals would eat their dust all the way across the Chilcotin. It didn't take long for the suckers in the van to realize they'd been out-smarted.

Traveling along, the fine powdery dust continually crept in around door linings, windows and vents. Soon, the occupants of the van took on a rather ghoulish appearance while suffering through endless sneezing attacks.

In order to see the road in front of them, the gals had to fall way back. After a while, they couldn't see any sign of the truck. And that was just fine with them.

Meanwhile, up ahead, the guys were making pretty good time. Then suddenly, they hit a culvert, and unbeknownst to them, the frame of the truck came down so hard, it sliced the rear brake lines in two. Bob tried to slow down for an upcoming curve and realized he had no brakes. Unable to complete the turn, he suddenly burst onto a side road. He continued on the new path until the steep incline of an approaching hill slowed them to a stop.

When they discovered the brake lines had been severed, Bob took out a pair of duckbill pliers, and with the aid of a rock, managed to pinch off the lines. The front brakes were still working, but would offer minimum braking power. Hydraulic fluid had leaked out from the ruptured lines so Bob quickly added some more. (He just so happened to have a can of hydraulic fluid in his truck.)

Proud of their quick repair job, the men soon headed back to the main road. They were certain the gals would be coming along at any moment, so they decided to wait.

Unfortunately, the gals had already passed them. They didn't even notice the remaining dust-trail that veered off the road.

After waiting thirty minutes, the guys were convinced the women had already gone by. Bob started the engine and they took off down the road once more.

Up ahead, the gals were searching for a dust trail. Sandy speeded up, thinking she'd lagged too far behind. Speeding down the bumpy road, the turbulent shaking increased so much, they all began to vibrate. They traveled faster and faster over ruts and rocks that were impossible to miss. Finally, Sandy figured out what happened.

"The men just wanted to get to Anahim Lake early so they could go fishing. I'll bet they're already there," Sandy said.

The gals were absolutely furious. Sandy speeded up even more while Phyllis and Shirley vented their anger. Their voices wavered in vibrating tones with each complaint.

"The nerve of those guys!" And, "They are so inconsiderate!" Then, "All they can think about is going fishing!"

Meanwhile, the men were saying the same thing about the gals: "They were very inconsiderate. They'd driven right on by. They didn't even slow down!"

The guys were becoming more and more perturbed with each mile they traveled. So Bob speeded up. When they approached an upcoming curve in the road, Bob quickly geared down, so the compression would slow them. Then, he applied the front brakes, and they fishtailed around the curve. Hurriedly, he accelerated again to regain their speed. The guys just couldn't wait to catch up with the women.

Speeding over the bumpy dirt surface as fast as they could, the women were still fuming. They were being tossed about in a dirty van with kids, and the men were enjoying themselves fishing. After several miles of violent shaking, the road was taking its toll on the van. It started rattling in places it had never rattled before. The gals were setting a new Chilcotin record for speed.

Then, the thought entered Sandy's mind that perhaps the men had stopped somewhere, without them noticing. But where?

Just then, Sandy saw a Native man riding on a horse leading a large bull by a rope. She decided to hit the brakes. The van came to a screeching halt while distributing a billowing dust cloud all over everything in sight. It was several minutes before the dust settled and the Native man could be seen once more. Disturbed by the intrusion, the man waved frantically as he tried to clear the air. He was covered in dust, everything from his hat to his horse, and the poor guy coughed and sputtered. The man was obviously upset and even the bull seemed irate.

Finally, Sandy spoke to the man. "Have you seen a green Ford truck with a camper on back?"

The man thought for a moment. "No. No cars."

"This was a green truck," Sandy explained.

"No. No trucks," the man yelled.

"Oh, no!" Sandy said, "We must have passed the guys. But where?"

They considered their options. If the men had problems with the truck, they may have flagged someone down for help. Maybe they were traveling in another vehicle. If they went back looking for them, they might pass them again. There wasn't one dusty body in the van willing to backtrack. The men were on their own. They would go as far as Anahim Lake and wait for the guys.

Meanwhile, the guys were still speeding along looking for any sign of a white van. They were setting their own speed record.

Several hours had past since they last saw the van. Now, they were getting worried. Perhaps the women and kids had broken down somewhere and they were traveling away from them. The gals could be stranded somewhere on the Chilcotin.

Just then, Bob spotted a Native man on a horse leading a bull by a rope. He quickly geared down and the compression slowed them. Finally, he hit the brakes.

When the dust settled and everyone stopped coughing, Gary climbed out of the truck and walked toward the man. Right away, Gary noticed the bull had a rather mean look on his face. Large amounts of dust had gathered in the corners of both eyes, along with an abundance of tears washing the dust out. Muddy tears streaked the bull's face. The bull appeared to be crying, as did the man. Looking at the horse, Gary couldn't tell what color it was, but its current shade was dusty-gray.

"Have you seen a white van pass by?" Gary asked.

"No. No trucks," the man said, waving his arm.

"Not a truck, a van," Gary reiterated.

"No. No cars," the man said in a grouchy voice.

Gary returned to the truck. The men held a little conference while considering their options. The women could be behind them, broken down, but how far behind? If they went back to find them, they could miss them somehow. Besides, they didn't have very good brakes, and they weren't willing to give up one inch of the road to backtrack. It was unanimous, the women were on their own. They would travel on to Anahim Lake and wait for them.

When the men finally arrived at Anahim Lake and managed to stop, there was lots of explaining to do. Everyone looked a little ruffled, including the poor dog who'd been gyrated, vibrated and up-ended so many times, he wanted to bite someone.

After a few minutes of everyone trying to talk at the same time, they all calmed down a bit and realized they still had a major problem. The truck didn't have the best of brakes, and they were headed for one of the steepest grades known to man. Too exhausted to face such a problem, everyone agreed they would have to deal with it in the morning. For now, they just wanted to rest.

By morning, they felt no worse for wear from the previous day's activities, so they made the decision to go as far as the Hill, then figure out what to do next.

By the time they reached the Hill, the truck engine had quit running. A decision was made that Gary would tow the truck down the Hill. Bob would steer it while keeping it in gear, and the truck would act as a drag for the van.

When Shirley heard the plan, she refused to let Bob ride alone. There was lots of discussion about it, but Shirley held firm and climbed into the truck with Bob. They started down the Hill.

The kids closed their eyes, and everyone held their breath. But right away, Gary figured out the drag was great. He didn't hardly have to use his brakes at all. For Bob, it was a constant battle to keep the shift lever from jumping out of gear. It took both hands and a lot of strength just to hold it in place.

Finally, everyone arrived safely at the bottom of the Hill, and a heavy sigh of relief was heard by all.

The procession continued down the valley while Bob and Shirley still rode in the truck. Looking out, all they could see was a giant wall of dust surrounding the truck on the outside, that gradually filtered through to the inside. Riding in the cab was similar to being on the inside of a huge vacuum cleaner, sucking up every bit of dust it could find. They both suffered endless sneezing attacks that brought tears to their eyes.

Two hours later, they stopped at the Crown Zellerbach house. When the two occupants of the truck crawled out, they looked like they'd been dipped in a flour barrel, and they both had blackened eyes from muddy tears.

Phyllis jumped out of the van and took a picture. Bob and Shirley had passed the test.

Dave couldn't wait to talk to Bob. He had a question for him.

"How many flat tires did you repaired coming across the Chilcotin on your $4 tires?"

"Not even one," Bob replied. "But I did have a couple other minor problems."

The road was never easy. It had the ability to chew up and spit out vehicles with such a brutish force, it made one ponder the power of the beast. And, the continuous supply of lost mufflers and tailpipes along its course paid homage to the beast.

It was common to find abandoned vehicles along the Chilcotin trail. The owners had given up on their vehicle and had given up on the road. These abandoned remains were eventually dismantled by motoring vultures of the Chilcotin.

I once saw a sign on a tree that said, "Bella Coola or Bust". A little ways further, there was an old truck pushed off the road with another sign: "BUSTED".

Each new season brought new road conditions. In the summer, it was the endless dust and bogholes. In the winter it was snow, ice and freezing temperatures. Fall brought lots of all the above, and spring brought the dreaded breakup with its many frost boils and mud.

In 1966, Graham Hall had the privilege of helping his brother-in-law Cecil Stacy move to the Valley from Vancouver. The two men traveled with an old truck loaded to the hilt with all of the Stacy's belongings, including a very heavy piano. There was so much stuff, the load reached well above the side boards. Graham knew the trip across the Chilcotin with an over-loaded truck wasn't going to be easy. Cecil had no idea what lay in store. He'd never seen the Chilcotin.

Cecil and his German Shepherd rode in the big truck while Graham drove his Chevy panel. It seemed to take forever just to get to Williams Lake by way of the perilous Fraser River Canyon. Graham continually followed the over-loaded truck, making sure nothing important fell off.

Quite often, road work halted traffic for most of the day.

When the men finally reached Williams Lake, they rested for a few hours, then set out for the Chilcotin.

They traveled over endless potholes and ate dust hour after hour after hour. They traveled along at twenty miles per hour most of the time, but slowed down some when they shared the road with several herds of cattle. Finally, they reached the top of the Hill where they stopped.

By that time, Cecil and his dog were so covered in dust, it was hard to tell which one was which. Graham proceeded to warn Cecil to shake the dust from his clothing before starting down the Hill. The dusting ritual was to insure not having a sneezing attack while descending the 18% grade.

Getting underway, Graham continued to follow behind the large truck. He watched as the truck bounced over rocks covering the road. The trip was almost over and Graham was anxious to get home.

When they reached the halfway point at Upper Young Creek, Graham stopped again, this time to check on the load. Cecil's first glimpse of the Hill had left him with a dazed stare. Quickly, he exited the truck and ran for some bushes.

Graham knew Cecil hadn't seen anything, yet.

Further down the Hill, the road became more narrow, with solid rock on one side, and a bottomless canyon on the other. When they came to the first narrow switchback, Cecil had to maneuver the truck back and forth several times just to get it around the curve. Then, he repeated the same performance at the next switchback, but seemed to gain confidence as he suddenly

173

speeded up. Furniture started bouncing three feet high while a steady stream of dust sprang from the huge truck tires. Viewing it from behind, Graham was sure Cecil had lost his mind.

When Cecil approached the steepest part of the Hill, he continued his fast speed. Graham watched in horror, expecting Cecil to loose the truck over the side of the mountain at any moment. Graham was in a hurry to get the trip over with, too, but this was ridiculous.

Up ahead, the truck swayed as it flew around a slight curve, but righted itself, then slowed down some just before the last switchback.

It turned out the engine had stalled coming around the second switchback. That meant Cecil had no power steering and no power brakes. He had managed, after a hellish few minutes, to get the truck re-started just as he made the last turn on the Hill. Reaching the bottom, Cecil brought the truck to a screeching halt.

Immediately, the truck door flew open and Cecil jumped out. Hanging onto the truck door, he got sick to his stomach. When he recovered enough to walk, he crawled to the side of the road, sat down and cried.

Two hours later, the men arrived at the Hall's home.

That evening, Graham listened as Cecil told Angela and Star about their trip, and what he thought about the Hill.

"Not bad at all," he said. "Small things like a one-lane trail on a dangerous cliff doesn't phase me. I'm used to danger. I'm an ex-cop."

"That may be so," Graham thought, but he couldn't help noticing Cecil's eyebrows were two inches higher than normal, and the pitch of his voice had changed three octaves.

At times, we heard stories about Bella Coolans yearning to make the trip across the Chilcotin, but they couldn't get any further than the Hill before getting sick from all the dust. After several failed attempts, Barbara Gurr finally made it as far as Williams Lake. She stayed with Lige and Isabell and saw television for the very first time. She was 14-years-old at the time, and upon her return to the Valley, she informed everyone how awful it was to watch someone get killed on television. She felt terrible for weeks after witnessing a fabricated death.

Soon, other residents managed to venture out, wanting to see what this television stuff was all about.

People never traveled the road during breakup unless they absolutely had to. There were horror stories of bottomless pits of mud known as "Chilcotin quicksand". In some stretches, it was common to find tall warning poles sticking up at the edge of the road. They proclaimed: "Take heed, this one's a lulu." And, if you were smart, you tried to avoid it. One boghole was so deep, a 12-foot pole lowered into the middle completely disappeared out of sight.

Jackpine was the favored punching for bogholes. With each new breakup there were new pits of mud to be punched.

There were no reststops or bathroom facilities for three hundred miles while crossing the Chilcotin. Not a big issue, considering all the outdoor privacy, but hordes of mosquitoes were always just waiting for a broad expanse of bare skin to reveal itself.

A Native legend explained why there were so many mosquitoes in the area:

Mosquito was originally a huge monster that lived on blood. The monster liked to sneak around at night and carry people away. Tired of the monster's tricks, the people decided to destroy him, so they devised a plan. They built a big fire and laid around it, pretending to be asleep. When Mosquito came, they all jumped up and pushed him into the fire. He burned nicely, turning into black smoke. But then, to their horror, the smoke started turning back into Mosquito. They started blowing at Mosquito and they blew him to bits. Millions and millions of angry, bloodthirsty little bits, wanting to get even with everything in sight.

Anyone stopping on the Chilcotin plateau in the summertime knew the legend as absolute truth.

Fresh air facilities behind a bush became a common practice whenever someone had a nature call. To survive the giant mosquitoes, people often carried a tree branch with them to swat at the giant insects as they squatted. This method was referred to as "squat and swat".

When Sally (not her real name) was traveling the Chilcotin road with her husband, she needed to go so they stopped. She soon disappeared into the trees with her switch and found a private spot.

She dropped her pants down to her knees, while maintaining a steady discharge of swats. Then she squatted, but in mid-squat, she felt a bite and instantly swung at her assailant. Being perched on the slope of a hill, Sally suddenly lost her balance and fell over backwards. She began to roll end over bare end down a steep thirty-foot drop. With each roll she seemed to pick up speed. During one of her maneuvered rolls, her pants caught on a bush and were jerked off from her.

Stripped and shaken, Sally landed at the bottom of the hill. All she could do was cry. Looking up, she saw her pants hanging from a bush. In her horror, she turned red with embarrassment.

Sally crawled slowly up the hill to get her pants. She was fearful of another fall should she try to dress so she continued to climb the hill half naked. (This made the mosquitoes very happy.) Finally, she reached level ground once more and put her pants back on.

Sally dusted herself off and felt fortunate just to be alive after the frightening ordeal. Her pride had been severely crushed but everything else seemed intact. Gradually, she made her way back to the car.

Her worried husband soon met up with her and asked, "What took so long?"

Sally didn't want to explain what really happened, so she said, "The mosquitoes were just awful. It required lots of swats."

"Boy, the mosquitoes must have been bad," her husband said, looking at the back of her pants. "One bit a hole clear through your pants, and another one ripped a pant leg half off."

11

Living with the Bears

After playing at weekend dances, Johnny often took long walks to the Bella Coola river in total darkness. The rich scent of moist vegetation filled the night air. He never carried a flashlight, but his eyes gradually adjusted to all the tree shadows that took on strange forms. Occasionally, a bare branch would tug at his jacket and he would sweep it away. As Johnny walked along, he was constantly drawn to the rushing sounds made by the river.

Being musically talented, Johnny thought the river had wonderful symphonic tones. Low base rumblings were created by heavy boulders tumbling slowly along the bottom. On the other bank across the river, there were chord-like gurgling sounds. There were cymbal splashes as water hopped over semi-exposed rocks, and high-pitched rustlings as the wind whispered softly through the evergreens. The beautiful symphony that played nightly at the Bella Coola river was a melodious treat to his musician's ear.

Then Johnny learned about the many grizzly bears who visited the same area after dark. Evidently, the bears enjoyed the symphony too. When Johnny found a huge track covering his own, he decided his symphony should be conducted during daylight hours, and perhaps with a gun close by.

I once asked an old-timer how many bears he thought there were in the Bella Coola Valley during salmon season.

"There's about as many bears as there are people," was his reply.

"How many people do you think there are in the Valley?" I asked.

"Maybe 1200."

One bear for every person. I didn't know how accurate his figures were but they sounded reasonable to me. Everywhere I went, I heard stories about the Pacific Northwest bruin with its enormous appetite and unpredictable ways. But, what amazed me most was how many different kinds of bear there were in the Valley.

If someone planted a garden, then suddenly a garden variety appeared to trample and uproot the plants. If someone planted berry bushes, then a berry bush variety showed up to help harvest the crop. An orchard produced a tree variety that not only stripped the trees of all the fruit, but managed to prune the branches as well when they broke under its heavy weight.

Fisherman often saw a fish variety while fishing the river, and even a thief variety that sometimes stole their catch. There was a variety that liked to blow snot on dogs when they got a little too close, and this special breed was given the nickname "Snotdogger".

There was an old lazy variety that enjoyed hanging around the garbage dump called a "Dump-bum" and for homes without a dog to protect their yard at night, there was the front porch or yard variety. All varieties of bear had one thing in common. They were a big nuisance.

179

When I visited at different homes in the Valley, I stopped asking about any crops people might be trying to raise. I knew better than that.

"So tell me, what variety of bear are you accommodating this year?" I would ask.

Valley folks had developed a good sense of humor about the over-grown pest that often showed up at their barns, creeks, orchards, and sometimes their homes. But big, pesky bears presented a unique problem, because they were so unpredictable.

Intrigued by the Bella Coola nuisance, I started reading everything I could find about the animal. I talked to many old-timers who'd dealt with them first hand, over a long period of time. I learned many interesting facts about the grizzly and black bears roaming at will in the Bella Coola Valley.

I found that Grizzly bears average 600 to 800 pounds in weight, but occasionally tip the scales at 1,000 pounds. They have a claw design and shoulder hump muscles for digging up roots and small animals living underground. Grizzlies can digest a wide variety of foods.

Body features are usually distinguishable from black bears by the shoulder hump, dished face, longer claws and lower head carriage. The low head carriage brings more swagger to the grizzly's walk. Grizzlies generally come in shades of blond, brown or black.

Black bears rarely go over 400 pounds, but in some areas, males can reach up to 600 pounds. Their diet is much like the grizzly's, but black bears have evolved as a forest animal, and have retained a sharp hooked claw for tree climbing defense. Black bears compete with grizzlies for vegetation and fish, but they don't have the digging ability that grizzlies have.

Black bears' ears are longer and more pointed than a grizzly's. They also have a straight or roman-nose face profile and higher head carriage when walking. They are generally black in color but also come in varying shades of brown.

Grizzly cubs stay with their mothers anywhere from two to four years. Black bear cubs only get the sow's mothering for one and a half years, making them very vulnerable during their first year away from their parent.

The surrounding coastal rain forest of the Bella Coola area provided the nourishment and genetics to produce immensely large grizzly bears. The area was well known to trophy hunters because the Boone and Crockett Club lists have always been dominated by world class grizzly bears from this area. Over 50% of the top 10 largest grizzlies in the world have come from this region. So, when speaking of the Bella Coola nuisance, the one that plagued every home in the valley at one time or another, I should mention that it was usually a very large nuisance.

Being an avid hunter, Gary couldn't wait to have a bear rug hanging on his wall, so he hunted for several months looking for just the right bear. Being picky paid off, but the long wait took a strange twist. After spending countless hours hiking along dangerous bear trails in isolated terrain, Gary was amazed when the bears literally came knocking at his front door. All he had to do was frame out a cabin on his new property.

The Bella Coola River flowed through Gary's property on the north side. There was an old barn plus some fruit trees where he built his cabin. Many stories linked giant-sized grizzlies with the place, inciting some old-timers to refer to the area as Bear Wallow.

An early settler named Jim Holt had once owned the property where Gary and Sandy now called home. Jim was walking along a creek one day with his two dogs, while carrying a gun. Suddenly, a huge bear appeared from nowhere and attacked him. Jim quickly brought his gun up to shoot, but it jammed when he went to load a shell. The bear knocked him down with a powerful paw. Using his gun for protection, Jim held the gun crossways in the bear's mouth. The savage teeth were held back by the gun as the bear continued its attack.

The two dogs barked wildly and constantly nipped at the bear who was attacking their master. The bear continued its assault on Jim's body, severely wounding him on his thigh. The dogs kept nipping until the bear was temporarily distracted. Finally, after a hellish few seconds, Jim managed to get a shell into his gun. He shot the bear.

Jim's leg had been cruelly punctured so many times by the bear's teeth, his upper leg resembled ground hamburger. Fortunately, he wasn't bleeding too badly. Searching the ground, he soon found a stick to use as a cane.

Gradually, Jim made his way back to his cabin. In his hand he gripped the chewed up gun. It had protected him from further injury, acting as a barrier between him and those savage jaws of death. In the end it had killed the bear. Looking down at his two dogs, Jim knew they'd saved his life.

It had been several years since Jim Holt had owned the property, but things hadn't changed much. There were still lots of bears.

- Living with the Bears -

Gary moved his family into their new cabin before it was completely finished. He still needed to install a large picture window in the living room. In the meantime, he nailed peg-board over the opening.

One day, while they were away from home, they had a visitor of the snoopy bear variety. The bear easily removed the peg-board covering the opening, and took a tour of the new dwelling. While sniffing about on the inside of the cabin, the bear took a huge bite out of a sofa cushion. Evidently, the foam rubber in the cushion didn't agree with the bruin's digestive track. The bear soon threw up on the living room floor, leaving a large heap of fish-slime remains mixed with sofa chunks.

The pungent pile served as a "welcome to the neighborhood" when Gary and Sandy returned home. Their six-month-old German Shepherd who was suppose to be guarding the place was nowhere in sight. Finally, he was discovered beneath the cabin where the bear had chased him. After that, the dog headed for the crawl space at the slightest whiff of a grizzly bear.

After Gary installed the window, he awoke one night to hear a strange noise coming from the front porch, so he climbed out of bed to check on the disruptive clamor. Half asleep, he stared at the living room picture window that was now producing a strange shadow. The shadow was an outlined image of a bear with its paws stretched to each corner of the window frame. Looking at it, Gary thought his dream of a long awaited bear hide was just that--a dream. Visualizing a bear rug hanging on the window meant he'd spent far too much time thinking about it.

The next night Gary checked on the same disruptive noise. Then he realized the bear was for real and getting just a little too close. He had two small children who played on the porch, and out in the yard during the day. So, the window frame variety soon became a wall variety and the Shelton household didn't have anymore sleepless nights. That is, until an orchard variety showed up and started pruning their fruit trees; and a fishing variety constantly made splashing sounds in a nearby creek.

Gary and Sandy continued to live and build fences on their property. The bear encounters increased, and in time, they realized a well-trained dog was the answer to keep the bears at a safe distance. But even a dog could present problems, especially if, in a hasty retreat, the frightened animal brought a bear back to its master. We heard many stories about that very thing happening.

In the 1940's, an ex-hockey player named Connie King had taken up ranching in the Bella Coola area. King was in the upper Valley one day driving his jeep up the narrow road. He had his small daughter and pet collie with him.

Suddenly, the dog jumped from the jeep and ran to a nearby creek. Standing in the creek were five grizzly bears of varying sizes. The collie managed to stir the bears up with its steady barking. Then, the dog nipped one on the foot.

The huge grizzly lashed out at the collie, and right away, the dog realized it had bitten off more than it could chew. The frightened animal quickly retreated to its master with the bear in hot pursuit.

When King saw what was happening, he feared for his daughter, so he jumped out of the jeep, took off his hat, and started waving it. He could only hope it would scare the bear away. Lucky for King, it worked. The bear stopped, turned around and went the other way.

Sometime later, King had another incident with a bear. This time he wasn't so lucky.

There was lots of snow on the ground. King was out checking the feed on the winter range. He assumed that most bears would be hibernating, so he wasn't carrying a gun. When he walked toward a bawling calf, to check on it, he was surprised to find a silver-tip grizzly sow, with two cubs, just a hundred feet away. The bear instantly went for him.

King ran for a nearby poplar tree, but soon realized he couldn't get up the small tree. Quickly, he ran for a big spruce. The grizzly was on him before he could reach the tree.

King immediately started kicking at the bear. The sow bit into a boot and ripped it from his foot. Then the bear came at his face, and King raised his arm to protect himself. The bear savagely chewed on his arm then attacked his face. Still standing, King continued to fight the bear the best way he could. He tried to protect his face but at the expense of his arm. Then suddenly, the bear heard a cub hollering and turned to investigate the problem. King was surprised when the sow ran off.

King's injuries were severe. The temperature was well below freezing and most of his clothes had been ripped off of him. He knew he had to make it home as soon as possible or he'd pass out. On the long trek, King was forced to stop several times, but he eventually made it home.

Traveling by horse and wagon, then by jeep and finally by aircraft, King arrived at the

Vancouver General Hospital the next day for specialized treatment. One eye was missing, his nose had been mangled and torn open, and he had dozens of deep cuts on his arms, legs and body.

King lived to tell his story of the bear attack and continued ranching in the same area for many years.

Living with the bears was like having a poltergeist haunting daytime and nighttime activities to such an extent, everyday life had to be altered. Household garbage was the main problem and it had to be dealt with effectively or it would attract several unwelcome guests. The bears seemed unafraid of anything standing in their way, and their behavior was never predictable. Children had to be constantly watched and protected from the bears. Picnics and fishing trips to the river were rarely without incident as the uninvited phantom often showed up. Every tree seemed to harbor strange shadows as the Bella Coola nuisance continued to roam the dense forests of the Bella Coola Valley.

Every once in awhile I met someone totally unruffled by the creature that kept life so interesting. This was always a surprise to me. While talking to a local woman one day, I couldn't help wondering how she and her family had come to live in the Bella Coola Valley. She had no previous ties to the Valley and she was a city person by nature.

"It's like this," she said, "I picked up a map one day and chose the furthermost point away from my mother-in-law. Then I packed everything, including my husband and kids, and drove to the Bella Coola Valley to live without knowing one thing about it."

186

"Were you surprised at what you saw when you arrived?" I asked.

"Quite," she responded.

"But aren't you afraid of the bears roaming around on your property?"

'"No," she said, "I'd rather deal with a bear any day of the week than deal with my mother-in-law."

After hearing that, I sure didn't want to meet her mother-in-law.

For years, Bella Coolans had put up with the huge bears that lived in their Valley, and they dealt with the problem ones the only way they could, by destroying them. The Valley was where men worked, children played and where families raised their food. Early settlers found that once a bear became a pest, it was impossible for it to change its ways. Usually the problem behavior only got worse.

When Lige and Isabell were raising a large family at their Hagensborg home, they had a cellar variety bear that constantly went for the fresh cows milk cooling in the cellar. The milk craving bear figured out a way to get into the cellar no matter what they devised to discourage it.

They also had an orchard variety that continually came in their yard at night to get the fruit. Lige had to build a fence around the yard to offer protection for the kids from the bears.

One day, Lige was hunting in an area not far from his home. It was getting late and he knew it would be dark by the time he arrived home. Several members of Isabell's family would be at the house for dinner, so Lige thought he better hurry along. He determined he could take a shortcut through the orchard to save valuable time, and he figured he could jump over the little yard fence.

It was pouring down rain. Ever so often, lightening flashed across the sky. Lige started running through the orchard trying to build up some speed for his fence-jumping feat. Just as he reached a large apple tree, there was an electrifying lightening bolt that lit up the sky. Standing directly in front of him, blocking his path, was a huge bear. The bear was standing on its back feet reaching up in the tree. Lige was only 10 feet away and was about to run smack into the bear. All he could do was raise his gun and shoot.

The bear went right down and didn't stir. Lige waited to make sure the bear was dead. When a lightening bolt lit up the sky again, Lige could see the bear was no longer a threat.

Lige finally made his way to the house. Everyone was already at the table eating, so he quickly washed and changed his wet clothes, then he joined the family at the table. When everyone was through eating, Jim Mecham looked over at Lige.

"Are you OK?" he said, "You look kind of pale."

Isabell noticed it too and said, "He shouldn't have been outside in the rain."

"Well, by darn," Lige said, running his large hand over his head. "I just shot a grizzly bear out in the orchard, one that I almost ran smack into. I think it was a real big one, but it was so dark, I didn't get a good look."

Jim Mecham couldn't wait for morning light to find out, so he suggested they go out to the orchard with lanterns. The two men bundled up and went outside.

They found the huge bear laying at the base of the apple tree. Jim and Lige could see that the bullet had entered at the jawbone and had exited out the top of the bear's head. From the position that Lige had been holding the gun, that meant the bear was a very big one, towering well over his six foot plus frame. The men measured the size of the bear's head. It measured 17 inches between the ears. In all probability, it was a record class grizzly.

The next morning, Jim and Lige wanted to move the bear to a place where they could skin it. They tried dragging it with a horse but the large carcass wouldn't budge. One horse power just wasn't enough. The bear was so huge they didn't know what to do with it. They couldn't just leave it for fear other bears would be attracted to the decaying carcass. They had no other choice but to start digging a pit around and underneath the bear. It became an all day chore but eventually they covered the monster up.

There were other animals that presented problems for the Gurrs.

When they lived in the upper Valley, Isabell had a problem with the neighbor's horse called Nancy who was constantly getting loose and feeding on her vegetable garden. She'd chased the animal out of her garden many times.

One evening, while looking from the kitchen window, Isabell could see the outlined image of an animal in the garden. Quickly she picked up her broom and ran outside.

"Darn you Nancy. Get out of my garden," she said in her soft voice, and swung the broom at the uninvited guest.

As the animal moved toward the fence line, Isabell continued to follow swinging her broom.

189

Finally, the animal leaped over the fence. Returning to the house, Isabell knew she'd have to wait until morning to see what damage Nancy had done to her garden.

At daybreak, Lige was walking the fence line and noticed the large tracks that led up to the fence. From the tracks, he could see that the poor animal had landed on the other side of the fence, then slid on its backside for several feet before landing in the river. Upon closer examination of the tracks, Lige knew the animal Isabell had chased over the fence was a large male grizzly bear.

The bear must have been traumatized for life after its retreat from the broom-slinging woman, sliding down a long slope on its backside, then plunging into the cold water. But to be called "Nancy," well, that must have been more than any male ego could take.

Farming was next to impossible with the bears around so close. A local wilderness man named John Turner was farming in an area named after him, called Turner Lake. He went out one morning to do some work and decided he better take a gun with him. Walking along a familiar trail, he soon spotted a large grizzly just twenty yards away. At the same time, the grizzly saw him and charged. Quickly, Turner brought his rifle up and shot. The grizzly fell at his feet.

Taking a closer look at the bear, Turner knew it was a big one. It turned out to be a world's record in 1965, in the Boone and Crockett Club record book. The skull measured 17 inches in length and 9 10/16 inches in width--a total score of 26 10/16.

When Melvin Gurr was a boy, he was walking along the road and noticed the horses that were feeding in a nearby pasture. The grass was high and the horses had their heads down low. Melvin continued to walk on past them and when he looked back, the animals had raised up. It was then he realized they weren't horses at all, but three huge grizzly bears.

Mack Gurr spent a lot of time hunting for deer in the upper Valley around the Belarko area. On one hunting trip, he hiked into an unfamiliar area where steep snow-covered mountains came right down to the river, blocking his way. Unable to go any further, Mack climbed up a nearby crevice. It was 200 feet straight up, but he finally made it, and stood on a ledge looking out over the river. Watching for any sign of game below, Mack continued to stand on the ledge for another ten minutes.

Mack walked ten feet and stepped down to a lower shelf. On the lower ledge, Mack noticed a fir tree with its lower branches pushed way down by snow covering its base. Just as Mack reached the tree, he heard a horrific roar. Right away, he knew what it was.

Mack hadn't seen the sow grizzly laying beneath the tree. But he could sure see her now. She was coming right at him. Immediately, Mack stepped back toward the edge of the cliff, brought his gun up and somehow managed to knock the safety off. He shot and the bear went down.

As fast as he could, he jacked another round and shot again. But the bear charged him. This time she connected, slashing Mack with a powerful front paw and he was knocked backwards toward the mountain. Mack continued to clutch his rifle flat on his back, with his head laying downhill. Looking up at his feet, he could see the bear was coming again. Then she was right on top of him. Mack shoved the gun against the bear's chest and pulled the trigger. The blast up-ended her and she went over backwards.

Quickly, Mack jumped to his feet with adrenaline pumping through his body. The bear lay ten feet away but she wasn't moving. Suddenly, there was movement from the tree and Mack watched as two cubs ran out and stood by their mother.

Breathing hard, Mack reloaded his gun. He moved away from the cubs and slowly climbed back to the higher ledge. He started his long trek back down the mountain.

Walking along, Mack kept visualizing the attack and the strange circumstances that had led him to the bear's den. He'd climbed all the way up the hill, probably with the bear watching him. He'd stood for ten minutes on the ledge just above the bear then jumped down within a few feet of her. What luck!

When Mack returned to camp, he noticed hair all around the firing mechanism of his rifle and on the front sights. His coat was covered with red blotches where the bear had coughed frothing blood all over him. Mack knew he never wanted to see another grizzly bear, that close, as long as he lived.

In 1963, a Native woman named Mattie Jack was attacked by a bear while searching for stray horses in the Anahim Lake area. Mattie was alone, walking up a hillside when she spotted a grizzly sow with two cubs only two hundred feet from her. She made a quick decision to do just what the old-timers had told her to do under such circumstances: stand still.

The bear moved toward her and Mattie continued to stand as still as she could. Coming closer, the bear quickly veered off to one side, moving around behind her. The bear remained there for a few seconds then stood up on its hind legs and attacked.

The bear savagely bit at Mattie's neck. Still, she didn't move or cry out. Then the bear threw her down on the ground and started biting her shoulders and legs. It latched on with its powerful teeth and violently shook her until she lost consciousness.

When Mattie came to, she was terribly wounded and bleeding. She was covered over in a pit with dirt and mud. The bear had buried her with the intention of coming back to feed on her. Digging her way out, Mattie was able to walk a mile back to a tree where she had tied her horse. Eventually, she made her way back to camp.

It was a long time before Mattie's injuries healed. Fortunately, she survived her horrifying ordeal and lived to tell her story.

When the Mecham children were teenagers, two of them were riding a motor bike in the upper Valley when their bike broke down. They were stranded on a lonely dirt road. But it wasn't lonely very long, because three giant grizzly bears appeared on the hill just above them. Soon, the bears made their way toward them. Fearing for the worst, all they could do was clutch the bike and hold real still. Fortunately, it worked. The bears walked right on past them.

Bears seemed to be on everyone's mind all the time. When a local man climbed into bed one night, his wife wanted to know if the dogs were all right outside.

"Yes, they're just fine. I just checked on them and they're all three laying out on the front lawn asleep."

His wife quickly sat up in bed and said, "But we don't have three dogs."

Upon closer examination, the couple found their two dogs huddled together clutching the back porch. The dogs had been chased to the rear porch by three Snotdoggers who were now enjoying the front lawn as a place to sleep.

12

Cabin Fever

Bella Coola's sportsman paradise proved to be an extraordinary experience for avid fishermen. Responding to some primeval urge, sportsmen often left the security and warmth of their own home just to stand next to an icy cold stream, in icy cold weather, to catch (you guessed it) icy cold fish. It didn't matter what time of year it was.

The Bella Coola angler could catch Steelhead almost year round. Spring Salmon entered the Bella Coola and Atnarko Rivers in early May, and provided a great fishing experience. Catches weighing in at 40 to 50 pounds were not uncommon. Coho entered the river in September with the peak of the run in October. Sea run Cutthroat trout were present in the spring and fall, and Dolly Varden Char were available all year.

Responding favorably to their beautiful surroundings, men seemed to take on a warm healthy glow. They were convinced that Bella Coola's sportsman paradise was just that--a paradise.

For women, it was a different story. Each season brought new weather conditions and those conditions dictated if children played indoors or out. Even in good weather, children had to be supervised while playing outdoors, and small children required constant care. It seemed that women's work was never done. Often, chores became monotonous, mundane tasks requiring little imagination or skill.

The summer months were great. The whole family could go fishing, picnicking, hiking, and camping. And, there were times when outdoor activities lasted well into Fall. But when winter finally arrived with its lack of sunshine and harsh storms, families became house-bound for weeks at a time. In the small Valley, winter seemed to tighten its scope even further. Women sometimes felt they were looking at prison walls instead of beautiful mountains. For women stuck between the four walls of a tiny cabin, it was just a matter of time until those walls started closing in on them. And, it wasn't just the narrow walls of a cabin that came crashing in, but the narrow walls of the Valley as well. Compared to their all weather husbands with glowing faces, most women became listless and pale.

Usually around February or March, when confinement took its toll, the Bella Coola Hospital was besieged with ill female patients longing for warmer climates, new activities and new companions. The debilitating illness was called "cabin fever".

For Angela Hall, cabin fever struck suddenly one morning while frying eggs on an old wood stove that constantly belted out black smoke. Trying to cook the best way she could, she accidentally burnt the eggs. Having little food to waste, it was very upsetting. Living in a small 800 square foot cabin with seven people didn't help either. Angela decided it was time for a walk outdoors to vent her frustrations.

By the time she was warmly dressed and prepared to face the 28 degree temperature outside, she thought about making a quick stop at the outhouse. Opening the door to leave, Angela realized she couldn't go anywhere, because a very large black bear was blocking her way. Suddenly, her body temperature shot up and cabin fever set in. Angela started crying.

For Sandy, it was a snow bank that called her name. She'd been cooped up with kids for too long in a tiny cabin that was hardly big enough for two people, let alone four. She'd entertained herself by crocheting and knitting until her fingers were numb. She'd washed clothes on a wringer washer until she couldn't stand the sight of the old relic. She couldn't stand one more sibling argument. Finally, Sandy burst out of the door one day and leaping off the porch, she landed in a snow bank. Instantly, she started pounding the snow with her fists.

A passer-by might have thought she was diligently forming a lovely snow angel, but when she was through, there was no sign of an angelic design. Laying in the snow, Sandy knew that cabin fever had already set in.

For my sister Phyllis it was the lack of newspapers, books and cultural refinement that sent her over the edge. She couldn't live one more minute without those essential items to feed her ever-hungry mind. She yearned to attend a play or see a newly released movie.

For my mother it was the realization she was working in a cafe when she'd worked hard to obtain a real estate license. She was tired of baking pies and rolls, and cooking bland food for people who didn't enjoy spices.

Shirley was tired of moose meat, trout and salmon. She missed taking her kids to the A&W Root Beer stand for lunch, then to a park with no worries about bears. Shirley wanted to eat a hamburger at Foster's Freeze and make a trip to Disneyland.

The gals seemed dazed with cabin fever. Fortunately, they didn't have to be hospitalized for it. But there were those who did. Bed space at the local hospital dwindled as female patients checked in, staying as long as two to three weeks. The much needed rest from family and responsibilities helped them survive another winter.

I discovered I wasn't immune from cabin fever either. When it hit me, I found myself feeling lost in a maze. I wanted to go somewhere, but I didn't know where. I had so many responsibilities with the new baby, I oftentimes felt overwhelmed.

I tried explaining my strange feelings to Dave.

"I miss my horse, Tony," I sobbed. "He was my best friend and I miss horseback riding."

Dave replied, "You couldn't ride a horse right now. The snow is too deep. Besides, Tony was so old, he's probably at the glue factory by now."

I found one of the side effects of cabin fever was being unable to put into words what the real problem was for lack of knowing myself. Men seemed immune from its clutches, and often lacked sympathy for the condition that was driving most women half crazy.

Hormones definitely played a role in the cabin fever syndrome, but that wasn't anything new. I wondered what the medical world would say about such an epidemic condition. I could just hear a detailed explanation by an imaginary male doctor:

"You see these two charts here? Well, they show the difference between men and women. You see here, men have a steady unchanging line across their hormonal chart. It doesn't matter if they're 5, 16, 21, or 42. Their hormones don't fluctuate much. But now, lookee here at this woman's chart. It looks like a diagram for a roller coaster ride with all its many zigs and zags starting at a very early age and continuing on through each phase of her life. Women just have to adjust to the ever-changing female body."

Little hope of understanding coming from a male medical doctor, I thought, even an imaginary one. There just didn't seem to be any real help for cabin fever. Once it set in, there was no miracle cure to bring a woman out of it. She had to find a way to work it out on her own.

I could just imagine what the early Norwegian settlers had to say about their despondent women:

"Well, dis contray with eets fjords, it yist makes dem wemon crazy, Yah? De gremlins take de hold and day speak dat yibberish."

I pictured an anthropologist finding a prehistoric petrified skull and lamenting:

"Ah, this one is a female. See how the jaw is locked in a wide arc depicting a scream. She must have died while suffering from a common dreaded illness of that epic period. The scientific name for the disease is cabina feverous. Those poor aboriginal females suffered their dementia as a direct result of a lack of understanding by environmental changes that spurred human and cultural adaptation (mainly hunting and fishing companions). Homo Sapeins had to learn to modify behavior according to circumstances, and women living in small caves with their young children had little outside activity. When the temperature dipped well below zero, it only made cabina feverous soar to greater heights. Poor soles, too bad they couldn't adapt as easily as their active male partners."

Then I imagined what a Native man would say about his listless wife:

"Squaw no like teepee. She no cookum skunk, woodchuck, raccoon, opossum, and chipmunk for Brave. Me hold powwow with medicine man. He fix."

I knew that men weren't going to offer any help or solutions. Somehow, women had to fight their own battle to regain the knowledge that someday there would be sunshine again, and fun in the outdoors with the people they truly loved.

While pondering the condition of the female dilemma, I couldn't help being absorbed in my strange new thoughts. I kept reaching back in my memory to understand how I'd come to such a restricted state.

I'd always been very active. With motherhood and being a wife came new responsibilities. Even though I wanted to be a mother and wife more than anything else in the world, I hadn't planned on it changing my life to the degree it had. It seemed as though I was tied to the house. Even when I was away, there was an invisible umbilical chord connecting mother with child. My thoughts never seemed free of my obligation to my off-spring and husband.

I've always loved the outdoors. I was raised on a large ranch in California with horses, cattle and other farm animals. When I was 16-years-old, I built a large tree house high off the ground in an oak tree, just so I could have a place to do my school work outside. I remembered straddling a horse while reading a book for a book report. I had a special place which I called "my camp". It was on a hill overlooking the lake on our ranch. The lake was a half mile from the ranch house, and there were several ponds that dotted the landscape in every direction. I used to ride my palomino horse to my camp and spend the night. With a campfire ablaze, I loved listening to the French frogs, with their foghorn rhythms, as they crooned me to sleep at night.

Placerville was where I went to school. It was fifteen miles east of the ranch and the largest town in the area. Students traveled by bus from the summit above Lake Tahoe in the east, to Latrobe in the lower valley in the west.

I rode Bus #5 to school. It was an old conventional school bus geared for long hauls up steep canyon grades. Before catching the bus each morning, I walked a mile to reach the main road, called Green Valley Road.

All my friends were as crazy about horses as I was, and we often took part in activities like barrel racing and long trail rides. My horse was a good jumper and I enjoyed jumping him over a large water trough located in the huge corral east of our house.

The foothills of the Sierra-Nevada Mountains where Placerville is located is Motherlode Country. It was here that gold was discovered in 1849 in a little place called Coloma, just ten miles northeast of our ranch. When I was free of school in the summer, my brother Gary and I spent most of our time panning for gold. We had the gold fever bug in a big way. Even though it was hard work, it didn't stop us from turning over hundreds of pounds of dirt each summer, even in the severe hot temperatures so common to the area.

The ranch had numerous old mines like the Blue Dog Mine and the Sugar Pine Mine. We spent countless hours digging through tailings and rubble just in case something had escaped the original old-time miners.

There were two things we had plenty of on the ranch: rattlesnakes and poison oak. Gary and I both carried guns to kill the snakes every chance we got, and digging around in creek beds, we had plenty of opportunities to do just that.

I accidentally sat down on a rattlesnake one day while it was resting in a cool creek bed. I'll never know why it didn't bite me. I think perhaps it was asleep, wrapped around the bottom of a small round rock where I decided to seat myself. By the time I discovered the snake, I didn't dare make a move. I had to sit perfectly still for a hellish five minutes, waiting for it to wake up. When the snake finally came to, it gradually crawled off. I was shocked at its size. It was well over five feet. I watched in horror as fifteen rattles scratched the surface of my pants as it departed.

I enjoyed panning for gold. One day, as I slowly washed the sand back in my pan I was taken by surprise. I saw two beautiful gold nuggets, one the size of a bean and the other half its size. Along with the two nuggets were several small flakes of gold. I was thrilled.

After I graduated from high school, I started dating a young man I'd met in high school, named David. Our first meeting had taken place on old bus #5. David was finishing a three year stint in the U.S. Navy and was temporarily home on leave when we started dating.

It was seven months before we tied the knot. Then, one year later, we left for Canada.

I thought about the events shaping my life and leading me to this place. I eventually pulled myself together long enough to understand why I was lost in a maze. All I needed to do was find more time for myself. I could still spend time in the outdoors. It just required a little more effort and perhaps a baby-sitter. I also realized I needed to keep learning new things.

I completely recovered from my bout with cabin fever, and I felt like a new person when I finally put my life back in focus.

Then I felt guilty for being so harsh on my "imaginary men". I needed to apologize to the male medical doctor. After all, he was only going by the medical charts in his office.

I apologized to the anthropologist. I knew he was restricted by scientific information.

I said I was sorry to the Norwegian settler who was too industrious to know about cabin fever.

And the Native man...well, I was still trying to forgive him for the skunk and opossum.

13

APHOOOT!

I knew something was terribly wrong. I walked slowly down the wide corridor of the hospital toward the nurse's station.

"Gayle," I called, and waited. Finally the nurse appeared in the hallway.

"Something's wrong. I think this baby is going to be born right now."

"That's not the way it works," Gayle said. "How far apart are your pains?"

"I can't tell. It just seems like one long pain." I steadied myself and took a deep breath.

"Let's get you back to bed," Gayle replied.

"You better check. I think this baby is going to be born right now," I said.

"You still have a long way to go. You wouldn't be walking around if you were that close, eh?" Gayle held my arm and led me back to my room.

"I'll give a quick check to make sure you're OK, then you can rest for a while, eh? After a quick look, Gayle's expression changed.

"Aphooot, aphooot!" she said. Then she ran from the room.

A nurse's aid soon entered the room and I asked her what "aphooot" meant. It sounded like a technical Norwegian birthing term.

"She didn't say aphooot," she responded, "She said a foot."

I laid back and tried to understand what that meant.

"Your baby is coming into this world feet first," she explained.

Gayle quickly returned and informed me she'd called Dr. Chisolm who was on his way. The two women moved me onto a gurney and transported me to the birthing room. I wanted Dave to be with me, but he'd left to get something to eat. I also wanted Dr. Crosby, but he'd left the Valley to work in a large hospital somewhere in the province. By the time we reached the birthing room, the pain had increased to such a point it was almost unbearable.

"Don't push down," Gayle told me as she leaned over me. I took a deep breath. Inside my head I heard a little voice say, "Push".

"The doctor is on his way, just don't push down yet," she told me once more.

But the voice said, "Push down". I took a deep breath and started pushing.

Gayle called to the nurse's aid, "She's pushing. See if the doctor is here yet."

Once I started pushing, I didn't stop. Soon Dr. Chisolm arrived, and there was a scurry to prepare him for the delivery already taking place. Then the pain became so intense I passed out.

I don't know how long I remained in my deep sleep. When I finally awoke, I couldn't open my eyes because of a blinding bright light overhead. Laying there with my eyes closed, I listened intently for a baby's cry. Only silence filled the room.

"I don't think the baby made it," I told myself as a tear ran down my face then into my ear. I fell asleep once more.

The next thing I knew, there was a pressure on my chest. Slowly, I opened my eyes. I was relieved to find the blaring, bright light was gone. Laying on my chest was a strange little creature. The creature resembled the contents of a can of Spam.

Startled, I asked, "What is it?"

Gayle leaned over me. "It's a girl."

Suddenly, the Spam creature reeled out its long tongue. The sight was pretty scary.

"What is it doing?" I asked.

"It's trying to taste the new world it's come into, eh? It's a good thing you decided to push because the cord was wrapped so tightly around her neck, she was strangling. Dr. Chisolm had to work for quite a while to get her to breathe. She had to have oxygen, but she is doing just fine now."

I looked up at the Spam creature and watched as it reeled out its long tongue once more.

"What will you name her?" Gayle asked.

I had to think for a moment. Finally I remembered. "Chere'," I said. "Chere' LeNoir Foltz."

When Dave arrived at the hospital, he was surprised to find a new baby daughter. Later, when we had time to talk, we discussed how fortunate we were that the baby was alive.

I spent a week in the hospital after the difficult delivery. On the second night of my stay, a Native woman named Grace was admitted. She had traveled from the Anahim Lake area and was already in labor. She was placed in a bed next to mine. Sometime during the wee hours of the morning, I awoke to hear grunting sounds. A curtain had been drawn between us.

"Are you OK?" I asked. As I waited for an answer, I heard more grunting sounds.

"Are you OK?" I repeated, but the woman still didn't answer.

Finally, I got to my feet and moved toward her bed. When I looked around the curtain, I couldn't believe my eyes. Grace had delivered her own baby.

"I'll get Gayle," I offered, starting toward the door. When I met Gayle at the nurse's station, I told her the news. She promptly responded to our room.

I could hear Gayle's voice clear down the hall as she spoke to the woman. "Grace, I told you not to do that. What are you thinking of, eh?"

I returned to the room and crawled back in bed. I listened as Gayle continued to rant and rave. Finally, she had the situation under control and took the baby to the nursery. Dr. Chisolm was called to check on the mother and the baby. Eventually, things returned to normal.

On the third night in the hospital, I awoke around midnight to find a strange man standing in my room. He kept mumbling something and I finally realized the man was drunk. I started yelling for Gayle and she quickly appeared in the doorway. She was surprised to find the man in the room.

"What do you want?" Gayle asked.

"I come for Grace. She make me mad. I going to hit her," the man said.

"You're not going to hit Grace, she just had a baby," Gayle said, and pushed him back into the hall.

"She make me mad," the man said with slurred speech.

Gayle pushed him once more and he staggered backwards down the hall. Again, she pushed him. The man started down the stairs and suddenly fell. Gayle quickly closed the door to the stairwell, then ran to call the Royal Canadian Mounted Police.

I looked over at Grace who was sitting up in her bed. This brave woman who'd delivered her own baby, had tears in her eyes. I couldn't help wondering what kind of life she'd be returning to.

"Men!" I said, and shrugged my shoulders. Then, I rolled over and thanked my lucky stars for my good husband and my good life.

On the fourth night in the hospital, melancholy set in. I quietly laid in bed and watched out the window as silent snow flakes fell to the ground. Still fighting to regain my strength, I closed my eyes and tried to envision what lay in store for my family.

The Canadian economy was struggling. It had become very clear to me that it would be a long time before things improved. Lying there, I realized that change was inevitable. My time in the Bella Coola Valley was almost over.

As I continued to look out the window at the falling snow, I thought about the hard working people who'd founded a community on the good things of life: God, family and industry. The Valley people stood firm on these principles while the rest of the world seemed to rush toward any new philosophy. I pondered these things in my mind. Then, a wonderful feeling came over me. I was content just in the knowledge that there was such a place.

When I was finally released from the hospital, I was very happy to be rejoin my family. The difficult delivery had taken its toll on me, and it was along time before I felt like my old self again.

Sometime later, my sister Phyllis and her son Johnny left the Valley to move to Utah.

That spring, my folks left the Valley. Their work at the cafe had come to a standstill due to the poor economy. They returned to California where my mother could make use of her real estate license.

Bob and Shirley headed for the Smithers area, in British Columbia, and found temporary work. Eventually, they returned to California.

Later, Gary and Sandy and their family, along with Graham and Angela Hall and their family, made an epic trip across the Chilcotin for temporary work in Smithers. The morning they departed, three major events took place.

First, the weather decided to put on a real show by dropping lots of fresh snow and dipping temperatures well below freezing.

Second, Graham and Angela's rig, a Chevy panel, had engine trouble. Gary and Sandy agreed to make room in their pickup for seven more people plus their belongings. But there was no shell on the back of the truck to protect them from the bitter cold.

Third, the family cat delivered five kittens. No one had the heart to abandon a new mother, so a box with the mother and kittens was placed inside the already crowded truck.

The travelers found they could get up to six people in the truck cab (two were small children) plus the cats. It was a snug fit. The other five people had to ride in the back of the truck. To keep from freezing they wrapped up in blankets and a tarp. When the passengers in the back became so numb they could no longer move, they traded off with occupants in front.

The trip across the Chilcotin in search of work to support their families was a difficult one. The mother cat and her kittens arrived in Smithers just fine, as did the eleven people traveling by the only means they had available.

The Sheltons and Halls stayed in Smithers for several months. Eventually, they would move back to the Valley.

The old saying, "poor people have poor ways," dwindled to "poor people have no ways," as the economic slump devastating Canada was felt by all.

September 1967

Lonely and unemployed, Dave and I made the decision to leave the Valley and return to California.

Leaving our house was the hardest thing we had to do. All we could do was board it up with the idea of returning someday. We couldn't take much with us, just our clothes and our two babies.

Before making our final departure from the Valley, we stopped at the first switchback and looked out over the Valley. Then, we drove to the second switchback and noticed a man in a truck with a camper. He was pulled over so Dave stopped to see if he needed any help.

"Are you broke down?" Dave asked.

"No," the man answered, "I'm just waiting for my wife. She's walking down the Hill and should be here any minute."

Dave and I laughed knowing his wife wasn't the first person to walk down the Hill.

"I've wanted to see the Bella Coola Valley all my life," the man said. "I made it as far as the Hill once, but my wife refused to go down it. This time, we have an agreement: I drive to the second switchback and she hikes down the Hill. At last, I'm going to go fishing in the Bella Coola River."

Again, Dave and I laughed.

Just then, there was movement on the road above us, and we all watched as a large grizzly bear crossed the road, then headed toward the river. Quickly, it disappeared out of sight.

Shortly after, we heard running footsteps on the gravel as a woman came rushing toward us. We could clearly see that the woman was upset.

"Did you see that bear?" she asked, all out of breath.

We all acknowledged that we'd seen it.

Still out of breath, the woman stared at her husband. "If you think I'm going to camp out with that thing running loose, you're crazy. You can just take me right back the way we came. I'm not stepping one foot in the Bella Coola Valley now."

The poor man looked disappointed. He slowly strolled back to the truck where his wife was now sitting. Looking over his shoulder he said, "Maybe next year I'll get to see the Bella Coola Valley."

Dave turned the ignition key and we soon climbed the Hill toward the third switchback.

"Well," he said, "At least we got to see the Bella Coola Valley, and we managed to have two little girls born there."

Somewhere between the second and third switchback, I broke the news to Dave we were going to have a third baby, only this one would be born in California. Fortunately, he didn't swerve off the road. We continued on up the Hill to make our voyage across the Chilcotin.

Thinking back, we were just children when we arrived in the Valley. Now, we were departing as adults. It wasn't easy to leave the life that we loved so much, but with us we were taking a good foundation of what marriage and families are all about. Our experiences in the Bella Coola Valley had put us in good stead for our journey through life.

Over the years, whenever the turbulent fast paced world became too much for Dave and me, we could always reach back into the recesses of our minds and think of a long dusty road full of twists and turns, and many bogholes. A road standing the tests of time and mother nature. A vital link to the outside world, the road leads to a beautiful valley where time stands still. It is a place where people depend on one another. It is a place where folks still talk about the accomplishments and achievements of their community--and the building of a road.

We picture a room with kerosene lamps giving off a soft light, and a pot belly stove as it blazes away with its unique smells and sounds. The warm radiant heat provides a wonderful crackling sound while the snow falls gently outside. Friends and relatives are close by. As we bask in the warmth of this beautiful memory about a precious place and time, a wonderful feeling comes over us, and our minds are once more filled with peace.

Epilogue

The experiences we had in British Columbia helped form the cornerstone in the foundation of our marriage. Living amongst the industrious Bella Coola people for two years taught us valuable lessons in self-reliance. We learned to appreciate the true meaning of a simple lifestyle, and the importance of family and friends. Our house-moving experience gave us the courage to attempt projects beyond our limitations. We learned to depend on one another, and the woods of the Pacific Northwest taught a young man about survival.

In 1992, I retired from the California State Department of Corrections after ten years of service employed as an Office Technician. Before my career with the State, I was a school bus driver and transported four of my own children to school for several years.

In 1994, Dave retired after a twenty-year career with the California State Department of Corrections. He worked at five different correctional facilities in California, including San Quentin, and was a Correctional Lieutenant at the time of his retirement.

It didn't take long for us to decide where we'd spend the summer months of our retirement. Our dream came true, and once again we became voyagers of the Chilcotin.